## Advance Praise for Te

"Susan O'Carroll Drake's *Teacher Training with Jesus* is a practical, sacred tutorial for teachers. In 10 powerful, life-changing steps the author entices readers to grow from a good teacher to a great one by imitating Jesus-style instruction. Ms. O'Carroll Drake concludes each chapter with a P.S. (Practical Suggestions). If followed, these suggestions alone, would transform your classroom and you. There are hundreds of books and articles on how to teach like Jesus. This treatise drawn from the author's time in the classroom and time with the Master is innovative and indispensable for a seasoned as well as a first-year teacher."

Judy Turpen, Contributing Editor, *Teachers of Vision Magazine*—
official publication of Christian Educators
Association International, Anaheim, California

"Learning from the life of Jesus should be the goal of every Christian, but Drake has again taken the comparison to new depths in her latest book, *Teacher Training with Jesus*. Chapter by chapter, Drake suggests attributes of Jesus Christ and calls each of us to follow the example of the greatest teacher to ever live by offering concrete and realistic suggestions. Each chapter of this book is a challenge to higher commitment with practical ideas for the Christian teacher, yet, more than a self-help or motivational book, Drake has hit the mark of truly inspiring the reader to a higher commitment of daily living the Christ-like life in the classroom."

Sheila Rogers Gloer, EdD, Curriculum and Instruction,
Baylor University, Waco, Texas

"Teaching is perhaps life's highest calling, and Susan Drake's new book, *Teacher Training with Jesus: 10 Lessons from the Master*, will be a gift to those who desire to do it well. Drawing upon the methods employed by the ultimate Teacher, Susan engages her readers from the first page until the last. Each chapter is succinct—

perfect for the busy teacher and yet filled with thoughtful insights. This book will undoubtedly enhance the effectiveness of the teachers who read it to the great benefit of the young lives they touch."

Danny O'Brien, (former) Senior Pastor,
Grace Fellowship Church,
Baltimore-Timonium, Maryland

". . . powerful, inspiring, and thought-provoking. You can't escape being moved to action by the personal encounters presented in this book. Regardless of your background, you will be deeply moved and challenged by Susan's compelling, real-life stories. Each lesson is filled with engaging content that will cause you to look at life with a new perspective."

Don Hulin, Assistant Director for Textbook Development
Association of Christian Schools International,
Colorado Springs, Colorado

# Teacher
# Training
## WITH
# Jesus

## 10 LESSONS FROM THE MASTER

**SUSAN O'CARROLL DRAKE**

Foreword by Tony Campolo

JUDSON PRESS
PUBLISHERS SINCE 1824
VALLEY FORGE, PA

Teacher Training with Jesus: 10 Lessons from the Master
© 2018 by Judson Press, Valley Forge, PA 19482-0851
All rights reserved.

Formerly published as *Secrets of the Master Teacher: Unlocking the Power and Potential of the Jesus Teaching Model.* © 2010 by Thousand Hills Publishing, Baltimore, MD 21212. All rights reserved. Library of Congress Control Number: 2010926809 Drake, Susan O'Carroll.

Secrets of the Master Teacher: Unlocking the Power and Potential of the Jesus Teaching Model / Susan O'Carroll Drake. — 1st ed. ISBN 978-0-9827006-0-0

Many names and details have been changed to protect the identity of students, colleagues, and the school systems referenced by the author.

Judson Press has made every effort to trace the ownership of all quotes. In the event of a question arising from the use of a quote, we regret any error made and will be pleased to make the necessary correction in future printings and editions of this book.

Unless otherwise indicated, Bible quotations are taken from the New International Version of the Bible. Copyright © 1999 by The Zondervan Corporation. All rights reserved.

Scripture quotations marked NLT are taken from the Holy Bible, New Living Translation, copyright 1996, 2004. Used by permission of Tyndale House Publishers, Inc., Wheaton, Illinois 60189. All rights reserved.

The story on pages 64–66 and the dialogue on pages 97–99 was originally published in the magazine *Teachers of Vision*, the official publication of the Christian Educators Association International.

Interior design by Beth Oberholtzer.
Cover design by Lisa Delgado and Delgado & Associates.

Library of Congress Cataloging-in-Publication data

Names: Drake, Susan O'Carroll, author.
Title: Teacher training with Jesus : 10 lessons from the Master / Susan O'Carroll Drake ; foreword by Tony Campolo.
Other titles: Secrets of the Master Teacher
Description: first [edition]. | Valley Forge : Judson Press, 2018. |"Formerly published as Secrets of the Master Teacher: Unlocking the Power and Potential of the Jesus Teaching Model, ?2010 by Thousand Hills Publishing, Baltimore MD." | Description based on print version record and CIP data provided by publisher; resource not viewed.
Identifiers: LCCN 2018011442 (print) | LCCN 2018033113 (ebook) | ISBN 9780817081904 (epub) | ISBN 9780817015503 (pbk. : alk. paper)
Subjects: LCSH: Christian education--Teacher training. | Jesus Christ—Example.
Classification: LCC BV1533 (ebook) | LCC BV1533 .D73 2018 (print) | DDC 268/.3--dc23
LC record available at https://lccn.loc.gov/2018011442

Printed in the U.S.A.

First edition, 2010.
First Judson Press printing, 2018.

*Dedicated to every teacher
whose commitment to excellence
and personal sacrifice
have made this world
a better place.*

# Contents

# Foreword

Teachers are a heroic people, especially those who teach in public schools. When politicians, parents, and average citizens criticize public education and blame teachers because children aren't learning in school today as we did a generation or two ago, people simply demonstrate that they are unaware of how things have changed over the years.

Today's teachers can no longer count on support from parents. It isn't just a lack of parental involvement in homework either. When I was a boy, if my mother or father came to school, I trembled, knowing my parent would side with the teacher and that I was in serious trouble. In contrast, when parents arrive at school today, too often it means trouble for the administration and the classroom teacher rather than for the pupil. No doubt every teacher has some horror story about a confrontation with a disgruntled parent.

Today's typical American youth is attached to a screen from four to six hours a day—a great departure from previous generations. Excessive screen time hampers the learning process. What's more, as many sociologists will point out, online media teaches that information must be entertaining—and catered to increasingly shorter attention spans. No wonder teachers are often confronted with students who seem to be bored or turned off by the educational process.

Added to these factors are other challenges related to America's poor overall nutrition, increased transience among school-aged children (especially in our cities), and families in transition because of divorce and remarriage. Then there are the sheer financial straits in which many public-school systems find themselves—particularly in rural and inner-city settings where poverty means the tax base is low but the needs of the students are high.

Consider that [at the time of this writing] in the suburban township where my university is located the school board spends approximately $18,000 per student annually while just nine miles away, the Philadelphia school board allots just $8,000 per student each year. Money may not be everything in education, but when, because of lack of funding, students have to study in classrooms wherein the ceiling plaster is crumbling, textbooks are out-of-date, and computers are unavailable, we have to recognize that money does make a difference.

All children are created by God to be equal and they should be educated that way. The teaching work is a Christian calling—just as the author of this book, Susan O'Carroll Drake, sees teaching itself as a Christian ministry. Teachers in general are among the least respected and underpaid professionals in our nation. Yet their investment in the lives of our children, and in the future of our country and the world, has never been more vital. They need the support of politicians, parents, community, and the media—and they need the words of encouragement and guidance contained in this candid and compassionate how-to-teach-like-Jesus book.

Some Christians dismiss the value of public education as secular and therefore hostile to our faith. But Susan Drake embraces the spiritual potential of public-school education. She recognizes what many people do not: that God will never be absent from the schools as long as prayerful people of faith are walking the halls and ministering through example and education in the classroom. Susan exhorts her fellow teachers to heed the words of Francis of Assisi who is credited with saying, "Preach the Gospel at all times, and when necessary use words."

Christian teachers can so live their lives before their students and colleagues that something of Christ is revealed and the message of God's love is clearly communicated. We need teachers who will do this—and teachers need a book such as this one to exhort their spirits to learn first from Jesus and to strengthen their hearts in the ministry of teaching.

Author Susan O'Carroll Drake is a veteran educator who has taught in both inner city and suburban schools. In the thoughts collected in this book, she shares with candor and humor her own challenges, the challenges of her students, and how good teachers can unlock the secrets to great teaching through the Jesus teaching model. In these pages, fellow teachers will find a spirit of compassion, empathy, and encouragement that they need as they carry out their duties, looking to Jesus' life and teaching for wisdom, understanding, comfort, and hope.

Tony Campolo,
President, Evangelical Association for
the Promotion of Education (EAPE);
Professor Emeritus, Eastern University,
St. Davids, Pennsylvania

# Acknowledgments

Many thanks to so many:

Professor Jesus—for your strength and protection, unconditional love, sacrifice, teaching model, and inspiration.

Wolfie and Riley—for endless technical assistance and for allowing me to share your insights and stories. For recovering my digital files so many times, for your endless patience, and for being my beloved biological children.

Mommy and Daddy OC—for never giving up on me or this book! For your critical theological corrections, endless patience, and for being "my blood."

Bro. George—for making me laugh.

The Drakes—for rave reviews.

Misty, NoNo, and Patcy: my Drake teaching sisters—for your inspiration, support and for still loving me.

Fiona—for speaking truth, for editing, inspiring, listening, and loving.

Fiona (again) and Jeff—for throwing the best book party ever! You'll do it again, right?

Kelly, Cindy—for your friendship, support, prayers, and unparalleled editing.

Matthew J—for always "having my back"!

Chris and Noelle Hollingsworth—for recovering the manuscript when my computer crashed!

The teachers and staff of Rodger's Forge Elementary School, Dumbarton Middle School, The Friends School of Baltimore, and the Gilman School—for helping me remember how it's supposed to be done, for your enthusiasm, and for teaching Riley and the Wolf. Special thanks to Mr. Conty for freely sharing his Latin expertise.

My house church—for your prayers, support, and inspiration.

Dr. Mark, Carol, Matthew, Jonathan, and Philip Talamini— for richly blessing us and for allowing me to tell a small part of that story . . .

My mentors and the lights of my teaching life: Keith Anderson, Tammi Dorsey, Holly West, Bruce Durham, Lorraine Swaika, Gene Yahn, and Al Zelkind. All my colleagues at ACHS, NHS, and now THS—I love you all.

Jenny T—I'd be lost without you.

Rebecca Irwin-Diehl, Laura Alden, Lisa Blair, and the Editors at Judson Press—who made this book better and made it happen again.

My many spectacular students, aka "my biology children" (not to be confused with my biological ones)—you taught me at least as much as I taught y'all!

# Introduction

What makes a great teacher? Is it raw intellect, first-rate training, a broad knowledge base, honed instructional skills, enthusiasm, dedication, all of these things, or something more? What separates humanity's greatest teachers from those we encounter daily or profess to be ourselves?

Consider the long-lasting power that great teachers wield. Confucius taught a way of life that has lasted through many centuries. Buddha spread his idealism through the Orient and beyond. Students of Socrates took his lessons well beyond the borders of Greece. Jesus of Nazareth taught a revolutionary message that created a worldwide faith movement. And your teachers changed the world through you! Teachers hold a long arm of influence over their students, their communities, and their world. Their reach extends from here to eternity and can hinder or enlighten society. A case in point: consider the effective yet twisted teachings of Machiavelli and the regimes that learned his lessons well. Contrast the terror of Hitler's death camps with the social progress in India following Gandhi's peaceful protests. Both Hitler and Gandhi were ardent students of influential teachings, those of Machiavelli and the Bhagavad Gita, respectively.

We've all been students of someone. And if you think about it, we are all teachers on some level. Parent, preschool teacher, public elementary educator, Sunday school or Hebrew school teacher, scout master or den mother, athletic coach, tutor, professor, middle or high school teacher, private- or public-school educator, business facilitator, homeschool mom or dad, pastor, community activist—it doesn't matter where or whom you serve, your teaching will alter human history. But what kind of difference will you make? Will your teaching change the earth for better or for worse?

Can you identify the best teacher you ever had? Was it Mrs. Ceanfaglione from third grade, Mr. Bennett from fifth, or Miss Ellen from kindergarten? Maybe the best educator ever to cross your path was your preschool teacher, and it all went downhill from there. Regardless of whether you found your best teacher (BT) in elementary or graduate school, it's highly likely that your BT was also your favorite teacher.

What made your BT so good? Was it his or her enthusiasm and mastery of the subject matter, a storytelling skill, exciting lessons? Or did you sense that your favorite teacher really cared about you? If you examine the teaching style and methods used by your BT and the greatest teachers throughout history, you may find that they have a lot in common.

If you want to recognize great teaching or aspire to great teaching yourself, consider exploring the techniques and philosophies of the world's greatest teachers. What habits, attitudes, or techniques can you borrow from them to make you the best teacher you can be? When I asked myself that question as a Christian, I turned to the example of my favorite spiritual teacher, Professor Jesus.

Why choose Jesus of Nazareth rather than so many other great teachers? I chose Jesus, in part, because he chose me—I already loved him dearly. With easy access to the Scriptures, I could search the text looking for specific ways that Jesus energized his teaching and reached out to his students. I hoped to find specific, practical applications that I could copy—and found plenty! I later compared Jesus' example with that of other great teachers and found many commonalities. The ten teaching tips I've included in this book come directly from the Bible, yet they also appear in the lives and teachings of many teaching giants: Socrates, Confucius, Buddha, and my own BT, Mrs. Bond. Please join me as I share some of the treasures I unearthed.

The Bible references many names for Jesus: wonderful Counselor, Son of David, High Priest, Lamb of God, Eternal King, Israel's deliverer, Most High, Prince of Peace, Rabbi, the Alpha and the Omega, the First and Last, my Rock and my Fortress, Holy One, the Bridegroom, a strong Tower, King of glory, Wisdom, the King's Son, a great Light, the everlasting Father, Ruler, the Ancient of Days, Teacher—the list goes on and on.

Some of these names are mentioned by the Old Testament prophets. Others originate from his followers. Yet it is Jesus who assigns to himself a great number of these names. Perhaps it is through the names he gives himself that Jesus hopes to teach us about his nature and his mission.

Of the many names for Jesus, both secular historians and biblical scholars agree on just one. Both acknowledge that Jesus was indeed a master teacher. In secular conversation, if Jesus is mentioned at all, isn't it often a whispered curse or a concession to his teaching prowess? "Oh, yes," your friend says in a practiced reply, "I can't buy the idea that Jesus was God, but I can admit that Jesus was a great man and a great teacher. Of course, he's right up there with Socrates and Buddha."

Despite neither holding academic degrees nor benefiting from formal educational training, Jesus clearly was one of the most engaging and effective teachers of all time. Equally able to enrapture a crowd of thousands or to challenge individuals, Jesus taught with authority and wisdom. The environment in which he taught was irrelevant: a crowded street, the top of a mountain, a synagogue during festival, the living room of a friend's house, a garden rooftop, or around a fire on the beach. The place and the circumstances didn't seem to matter, but the message and the individuals making up his audience did. So eager were they to hear his words that the crowds followed him from place to place. So challenging were his words that lives were changed, lost, and won. So radical were his ideas that traditional social norms and entire nations were turned upside down.

Jesus used no desks or lab stations, no LCD projectors or whiteboards, no computer animations or YouTube videos, not even any books. He received no salary but relied on the generosity of friends. Even without these teaching accoutrements, he managed to captivate all he met and taught. In only three short years, Jesus taught with an effectiveness that resulted in generations of devoted followers, a new religion, and a world that would never be the same.

If only I could get into the mind of Jesus, or better yet, if he could get into my mind, and if his wisdom could become part of my teaching program, think what I could do! The amazing thing is that Jesus wants to get into our heads, and he invites us to examine and emulate his ways. Jesus planned for his followers to access the power to responsibly and positively change the world. He has given to some the gift of teaching (Romans 12:6-7) and has called all of us to serve God by serving the world. But how can we follow Jesus' teaching plan for excellence?

The Scriptures offer volumes of insight into the lifestyle and lessons of our Lord. The Old Testament prophecies predicted what Jesus would do, while the New Testament intricately recounts his activities, provides glimpses into his personality, and offers specific content of his lessons. Sometimes, Jesus even explains why he uses certain teaching tools for a certain audience.

Given these historical yet practical resources, the question for teachers to ask themselves is not "What would Jesus do?" but "What *did* Jesus do?" As the question changes from one that is hypothetical to one that can be reliably answered, we move into practical territory. Watch one. Do one. Teach one. That is the training method by which physicians learn the procedures that they will perform on you, their medical patient. Just hope that you are not the second part of that process! Clearly, physician training programs have discovered what many of us have not: Most people can best learn a skill or technique by first carefully watching it performed by an expert. Watch a master surgeon tie the knot before trying it yourself. Study the moves and stance of the Olympic skier before your own race. Carefully examine the way that the prize-winning gardener prunes rosebushes before hacking away at your own. Observe the techniques and patterns of expert teachers before lecturing to that class of thirty-four exuberantly energetic darlings.

Scripture provides a reliable and revealing account of what Jesus taught and *how* he taught—the master Teacher's keys to great teaching. We can spend years studying the Bible and reading books about Jesus, and we probably should, but we have less than a lifetime to watch and study his teaching before we have to do it ourselves.

So, this little book is an attempt to streamline the process, to take us to a place where we can examine and study Jesus' teaching techniques. By focusing on Jesus' teachings and his teaching techniques, we can learn (and practice) the methods employed by the most highly effective teacher of all time.

Each of the following chapters will examine a specific teaching tip taken directly from Jesus' example. Once you discover Jesus' teaching tips, hopefully you'll be motivated to begin the journey from good to great teacher! Despite my enthusiasm in pursuing this topic, please know that I approach it with trepidation, stepping lightly and warily into a task rife with risk.

The first risk is that of being presumptuous. Who am I, anyway, to analyze the teaching techniques of Jesus? Could a lifetime of studying under great and not-so-great teachers combined with a mere decade of teaching science in public schools prepare me for this task? Lord, give me wisdom.

Another risk I face is that of picking the wrong lessons or issues on which to focus. The choices I make may be tainted by my prejudices and personal experience. I could be misguided, missing the important stuff or emphasizing something that won't help you. Lord, please give me wisdom!

How did Jesus think? What made him so engaging, effective, and challenging? Why did crowds follow Jesus? What teaching methods did he practice and endorse? What specific lessons can be learned by studying the ministry of Christ? Finally, how can I use the knowledge from these lessons to benefit me in my quest to, like Jesus, become a master teacher? You may find that I will provide more questions than answers—and many of these issues won't be resolved until we sit before the throne, looking up into the loving eyes of the greatest teacher the world has ever known.

I pray that after perusing the ten lessons presented herein, you will be motivated to study the methods and mindset of this great teacher, Jesus. Will you study with the goal of becoming the best teacher you can possibly be? Perhaps you will find like-minded colleagues or friends who will accompany you on this journey. Consider forming a study group with them. Let's face it, all teachers need a chance to vent, to share ideas, and to encourage one another. Perhaps you could meet together to discuss one lesson a week or one per month and punctuate your meetings with practicing the insights and techniques revealed.

Each chapter/lesson in this study includes: Scripture references, an introduction to the chapter focus, sections entitled Learning from Jesus, Trying What Jesus Taught, Practical Suggestions, and a Study Guide. The lessons might make more sense if you read the Scriptures listed under the lesson titles *before* exploring the chapter content. As you read and study each individual lesson, you also might enjoy reading the additional Scriptures referenced within the chapter text. The practical suggestions that follow each lesson are simply there to give you some ideas on how you might apply or practice the lesson's focus/content. Some of these recommendations will be more relevant to a private- or public-school classroom or athletic arena, while others can be applied in a Christian Education context or worship setting. Hopefully, you will find ideas that you can practice wherever you serve.

You may find that you need time to process each chapter's content and might be more likely to practice Jesus' teaching model if you commit to just one or two of the practical suggestions that follow each lesson/chapter. Whether you study Jesus' lessons in a group or solo, perhaps you can use the study guide to direct your discussion with friends or colleagues. I pray that you get excited about teacher training with Jesus!

**LESSON 1**

# THE
# Potential
## OF
# Preparation

**Scripture Lesson:**
Psalm 139
Jeremiah 29:11-14
Luke 2; 14:28-32
Ephesians 6:10-18

*"Children today are tyrants. They contradict their parents, gobble their food, and tyrannize their teachers." —Socrates*

It's a sultry Sunday night in the O'Carroll household, and you would expect a relaxed, quiet evening, especially after the full day of worship and youth group volleyball games, but Mom's accordion is on full throttle. Every now and then, she throws in a few measures of the Beer Barrel Polka between the hymns and choruses. As far as I know, we're not even Polish. Mom is practicing for tomorrow—the start of our church's Vacation Bible School. She's not about to go in there to lead the music program unprepared. If the dust on the case is any indication, it has been a while since the accordion has seen the light of day or the neighborhood children who will sing along with this novel organ . . .

One can never underestimate the advantage of preparation and training. Without it, your hope for consistent teaching success is thinner than the meninges that cover and protect your beautiful brain. But even with the best teacher training and preparation, things can go wrong.

We still chuckle about the time my dad agreed to sing a solo at our church's evening service, accompanying himself on acoustic guitar. He practiced and practiced the well-known hymn until he'd memorized the chords and the lyrics, yet when it was time to perform, he just couldn't deliver. After the first line of the song, the lyrics completely eluded him, so he finished by strumming for a while and singing "la la la la . . ." Isn't it odd that my talented and fearless father, who could preach to crowds, man anti-aircraft guns in Korea, and boldly combat injustice on a regular basis could not sing "Jesus Loves Me" to a congregation who loved him?

"La la la la" was about all I could say at the end of a long, sheep-brain-dissection-filled day. The classroom still reeked of the formalin, which made my own brain feel a bit "fizzy," and I still hadn't put away the dissection pans and tools when one of my senior AP students appeared with a feverish and rambling question: "What would happen to someone or what would be the risks to a person if, let's say a person introduced some brain tissue to their mouth? Like, I mean, if maybe they touched the tissue just a little bit?" (Let's pause for a moment to let your own brain wrap around that. . . .)

With deep suspicion, I asked, "How did this person contact said brain tissue and was it from a sheep?" He replied, "If a theoretical person happened to *lick* the brain we dissected in class is what I mean." I whispered incredulously, "Would this theoretical "licker" maybe be you? Were you not here when we learned about diseases carried via neural tissue and did you forget the oral reports your classmates presented about prion disease?"

This was my first such conversation in my three years of teaching AP Bio. Prior to the moment of this conversation, I'd felt quite confident in my ability to deliver an exceptional AP Bio curriculum. After all, I was certified by the College Board and had completed their official AP Bio Teacher training program. My course plans always passed on first submission and my students consistently beat the national average AP exam scores. My students were mostly academically-driven seniors, with a few mature juniors thrown into the mix, and I trusted them all to do what I asked them and to use sound judgment. None of my training or experience had prepared me for this conversation!

Of course, I had to report the incident to the school nurse (who was understandably rattled and who put this student on a thinly veiled and disingenuously labeled "death watch"), and I absolutely needed to call the brain-licker's guardians. Each day thereafter, I anxiously waited to make sure that this guy made it to school ("No Creutzfeldt Jakob disease yet," I'd console myself). I know he survived until Prom because I saw him there and he insisted that we take a photo together. We both smiled broadly.

Oddly, the administrator to whom I also reported the incident wanted to know what I had done to prevent the licking episode. The Assistant Principal implied that I was somehow responsible for the brain-licker's errant behavior. He wanted to know, had I explicitly warned the students in each class to not lick the brain? Frankly, no, because with all my preparation and experience, that possibility had never occurred to me. And I venture to say that it would not have for anyone else. (But, for the record, I now do exactly that before allowing any students to participate in the sheep brain dissection. Just in case.)

Even the best training and preparation won't always keep you from disaster. Unexpected circumstances, panic, forgetfulness, a cocky attitude, inattentiveness—these are just a few of the things that might lead to trouble. You can hold impressive degrees and stellar recommendations—you might garner rave reviews from your teacher trainers, yet still experience classroom disorder, danger, or difficulty. You should be properly prepared and trained to approach your teaching mission. And yet, with all these things, you might still occasionally make mistakes and metaphorically fall down on the job. But that training and preparation can help you address the unexpected—to formulate an immediate and effective response.

You may find that to soar in your field, you need more than the standard teacher training and preparation—you need God's training, perspective, and Spirit-inspired preparation. Where can we find this?

We can explore the origins of this special preparation and training by looking at the life of Jesus—How did he become a master teacher? What were his qualifications and preparations? The Bible clearly identifies Jesus as present at and participant in Creation (John 1:1-3). In the Epistles, Jesus is credited with being firstborn of all creation and the one through whom God creates (Colossians 1:15-17; Hebrews 1:2-3). He is now acknowledged as ruler over all that he participated in creating.

As co-Creator with God and firstborn of all creation, Jesus might reasonably be considered the wisest person who ever lived. Why do even the followers of Christ often fail to acknowledge this? Is it because we have listened too long and too often to the skeptics who dismiss any religious belief as for the weak-minded? Or is it because the accounts of Jesus don't present him within our preconceived notions of the intelligentsia?

Perhaps if we begin to recognize Jesus as one who possesses superior intelligence, then we can more fully trust him. And if Jesus came to earth with the intention of teaching, then teaching must be a valuable and honorable career choice—a career worthy of the time and effort it will take you to prepare for it.

## Learning from Jesus

Did Jesus need any teacher training? Probably not in the contemporary sense—yet Jesus still spent thirty-three years experiencing and investing in humanity. Did Jesus rely solely on superior intelligence and supernatural wisdom, or did his experiences enhance his teaching? We have no evidence or record of Jesus' formal education, and so we assume that he had none, but a closer look at the few records of his early life is revealing.

Jesus was trained in the art of carpentry by his father, Joseph. This was a demanding job that required physical strength, prolonged concentration, and extreme patience. First-century tradesmen were successful only if they displayed both considerable skill and business acumen.

Jesus was born to a family that observed the Jewish religious traditions. His parents, from the line of King David, fulfilled all the requirements of Jewish law for their son. Eight days after birth, Jesus was brought to the temple to be circumcised (Luke 2:21). Every year, they traveled to Jerusalem for Passover (Luke 2:41). An observant Jewish family also would have trained (homeschooled!) their young son in the history of the prophets, recitation of the Scriptures, and familiarity with the temple prayers.

As a young boy, Jesus had a working knowledge of the Old Testament Scriptures and was capable of conversing with and questioning the greatest religious scholars of the day. Jesus loved to go to the synagogue, where he would study and discuss the Torah with the priests and academicians. Even as a youth, he reveled in their debates and amazed both his parents and the religious leaders with his knowledge of the Scriptures. During his teaching ministry, Jesus would quote the most applicable Scripture for any given lesson or circumstance. It's unclear how much of Jesus' proficiency and skill was acquired through oral tradition, written study, or his time studying with the temple scholars. Perhaps, since Jesus is God, Jesus had no need of learning the law that he himself had written.

In Luke 2, we read about a family Passover trip to Jerusalem. On the long walk home, Jesus' parents realize he is missing, and they return to the city, frantic to find him. Three days later, they find twelve-year-old Jesus in the temple, discussing deep theological issues with the teachers of the Law. Three days! Those poor parents—Mary must have been beside herself! Have you ever had a student who was intent on studying with you, nonstop, for days on end? Have you ever lost a child for more than a few minutes and felt the gut-wrenching horror of it? Young Jesus asks his astonished parents, "But why did you need to search? Didn't you know that I must be in my Father's house?" (Luke 2:49, NLT).

Throughout his relatively short life, Jesus' family was diverse, his community extended—his cousin was John the Baptist; John's father (the husband of Elizabeth, Mary's cousin) was a priest in the Jewish synagogue; Jesus mother was a teenager; and his neighbors were Egyptians, Israelites, and Romans.

Jesus' parents taught him to revere the heavenly realm. Their bodies were grounded on earth, but their souls were open to messages from above. Both Mary and Joseph were no strangers to angels and prophetic messages delivered through dreams. They not only listened to God's messages but also followed up on his commands, modeling belief and obedience. When an angel visited Mary with news of an impending birth, she simply asked, "How will this be, since I am a virgin?" Mary accepted the angel's explanation (which turned out to be rather shocking news of a great personal intrusion) without any further questions, stating, "I am the Lord's servant. May your word to me be fulfilled" (Luke 1:34,38). When an angel told Joseph to take Mary as his wife, he did as he was told (Matthew 1:20,24). Jesus' very life was saved by a dream—when Joseph was warned in a dream to take Mary and Jesus to Egypt, they left that night (Matthew 2:13-15). It seems that God is willing to use even our sleeping hours to accomplish divine purposes.

In short, the greatest teacher to ever live exhibited complete mastery of his subject matter, held practical work experience, carried a wealth of life-learned lessons, and was open to God's Word. We don't come into the classroom holding Jesus' supernatural qualifications, yet God has given us tools to prepare for our mission. And God continues to give.

## Trying What Jesus Taught

We can and must do our part to prepare—studying our subject matter, learning from teachers who have come before us, practicing the skills required for effective teaching, and becoming experts in our field of study. Once established, the work continues—preparing meaningful lessons; honing our instructional skills; and establishing a classroom, athletic field, home, or church-based environment that feels safe and conducive to learning.

Although much of our training feels like our sole responsibility, God has already planned an individualized teacher prepara-

tion program for each one of us. In addition to our formal school-
ing, our experiences and relationships mold us into the teachers
God wants us to be. He purposely placed us in the families of our
birth, the schools we attended, and the relationships in which we
engage. God positioned us in the communities where we live and
the environments in which we teach, preach, coach, parent, or
lead. It is God's Spirit who moved us to accept this mission and
consistently prepares, protects, and provides for us.

Once, after a particularly tough day, I went to bed later than
usual; there was so much to do. But when my head finally hit
the pillow, rest did not come quickly. My mind raced around the
day's troubling events. Everyone said that Scott had been taken
into the local police precinct for questioning. Scott was one of my
current students, and I had also taught him during his freshman
year. I knew Scott quite well and liked him, too. Apparently, Scott
was being held on murder charges. Something to do with a weekend party gone bad, a loaded gun, a disagreement on a crowded
porch, and the corpse of another teenager pronounced DOA. I
didn't want to believe any of it. And I had no idea how I should
react when Scott returned to class.

I began to dream, and the scene was so real—the classroom filled
with students and the dissection pans strewn in disarray across the
black-slate lab tables. Sunlight was streaming through the door that
led to the stuffy-hot greenhouse, and an elongated shadow spilled
through the door that led to the hallway. Feeling a sense of being
watched, I glanced up to see that the shadow was formed by none
other than Scott. His lanky frame filled the height of the doorway,
his face betrayed a lack of confidence, and he had a textbook tucked
up against his long hip. Whoa. I didn't expect to see Scott so soon.
What to do? In my dream I saw myself: I slowly moved away from
the boys I had been tutoring, immediately walked over to Scott,
stood on tiptoes to put my arms around his shoulders, and pulled
him into a hug. I thought I felt him gasp before I pulled away and
said, "Please tell me you didn't do it." And then I woke.

I'm not usually one to find the right words at the opportune
time. When I'm nervous, I babble, and I only mastermind a great

retort well after being blatantly insulted. In issues involving death, weapons, and incarceration, I suspect I am even more woefully challenged. So it came as a great surprise when I was completely prepared for Scott's unexpected appearance in my classroom the next day.

The scene was exactly as I had dreamed the night before—the lab setup, the students in the room with me, the elongated shadow, right down to the book tucked up against the young man's hip. I could have never thought to hug Scott or ask the question if I hadn't been forewarned. Finally, pulling away from the hug, I said, "Please tell me you didn't do it." It was Scott's reply that I anxiously awaited. "I *didn't* do it. The guy I went to the party with was the one who pulled the trigger. It's all a misunderstanding that I need to clear up with the cops. I brought you my textbook in case you need it while I'm gone. I could be away for a while . . ."

Strangely, I found that the textbook Scott brought me that day was not even signed out to him. What made Scott bring me that book? And how or why did I have that dream? Maybe God knows that I'm more open to the Holy Spirit during my sleeping hours than my waking ones. The weirdness of it all didn't hit me until much later.

Proper teacher preparation and training involve more than a degree, more than an in-depth understanding of one's subject matter, and more than skillful application of proven teaching techniques. These things are important and good, in addition to being necessary. Yet proper preparation and teacher training, at any level and in any subject, require more than the church, state, or federal government requires. *Your* teacher preparation and training began a long time before you decided to teach—it involves all your experiences, every relationship you've entered, every book you've ever read, every class you've ever completed, every mountain you've ever climbed, and (for some) every dune you've ever crashed. It involves conscious and subconscious brain activity. Some might go so far as to say that even your dreams can help prepare you for this mission.

# P.S. (PRACTICAL SUGGESTIONS)

When you have a few quiet moments, record some of the experiences, mentors, or formal training opportunities that have prepared and trained you to teach. Consider ways you can further use these gifts and thank God for the chance to serve.

What long-term preparation or training opportunities should you arrange? Do you still need to sign up for that summer continuing education class? Have you registered yet for the fossil dig in Utah, the local coach's clinic, or the church retreat? Is there a grant deadline looming or an application you should complete and submit?

Psychologists and sleep scientists tell us that our dreams often feature the last thoughts we had before drifting off to sleep. Can you use that critical time to direct your thoughts to God in prayer?

Consider what you should be doing to prepare for this week and for tomorrow. Are you prepared for your classes and well-versed in what you need to teach? Are your materials ready and your labs prepped? How can you better plan so that you feel excited and ready to teach?

Keep a pad and pencil or pen next to your bed. When your mind is running, keeping you from sleep, and you think of things you need to do the next day, jot them down so you can relax and get some rest.

Determine what you can do ahead of time to prepare for the following morning: make lunch so you can grab it quickly in the morning, put important papers in your briefcase, and maybe pack your car before bedtime.

Consider subscribing to periodicals that will keep you abreast of the radical changes in your subject area or educational issues. Find time to occasionally catch up with an educational or subject-related journal.

Find and enroll in a workshop or class that is offered free of charge through your school system. Technology workshops or content-area classes can keep you current, preparing you for changes ahead. Find out what technology tools your school system will provide for your classroom.

Find a mentor program. Do you know any experienced master teachers, and can you learn from them? Investigate any teacher mentor programs that might be offered by your school or school system. Some school systems encourage veteran teachers to act as mentors to younger or less experienced staff. Incentives to participate may include recertification credits or salary grade advances. You may start in the program as an advisee and eventually serve as a mentor.

Tap into community resources. Investigate training programs and classes offered by local businesses, schools, outreach groups, zoos, or museums. Some may be free of charge for teachers, and others may be offered for a nominal fee.

## STUDY GUIDE FOR LESSON 1:
### THE POTENTIAL OF PREPARATION

**1.** Think back over your life, recalling your unique life story. Maybe review your résumé or academic transcripts to refresh your memory. Identify and list the ways that God has prepared you for your current leadership role.

**2.** What day-to-day preparations make your transition from home to work smoother?

**3.** Read Psalm 139. Which verse within this psalm do you find most meaningful? Explain.

**4.** "You hem me in behind and before, and you lay your hand upon me" (Psalm 139:5). To what personal circumstance might this verse refer?

**5.** Read Jeremiah 29:11-14, and then carefully consider the words of Job, "I know that you can do all things; no purpose of yours can be thwarted" (Job 42:2). How do these passages (Psalm 139, Jeremiah 29:11-14, and Job 42:2) relate? What comment do these verses make regarding your life's plan?

**6.** Read Luke 14:28-32. In this passage, Jesus uses a parable to teach the importance of careful planning. What do you identify as your greatest current stressor or challenge? How might careful planning allow you to better manage your greatest stressor or challenge?

**7.** Which practical suggestion(s) will you attempt this week?

**LESSON 2**

# THE
# Efficacy
## OF
# Empathy

**Scripture Lesson:**
Matthew 9
Mark 8:1-10; 9:17-28
Luke 17

*"I have been the whole day without eating, and the whole night without sleeping—occupied with thinking. It was of no use. The better plan is to learn." —Confucius*

God bless the Talamini boys! Matthew, Jonathan, and Philip Talamini were the sutures that held together our house church group. Willing and available to serve hour after hour, Sunday after Sunday, year after year, these teen brothers engaged with our young children while we (parents) socialized, worshipped, and prayed. Our Sunday afternoon meetings sometimes dragged into the night or were cancelled at the last minute, but the Talamini boys consistently watched and loved our kids. These boys didn't have to talk about the love of Jesus because they showed it by sacrificing their precious weekend time—time that they could have been sleeping, studying, or hanging out with friends. Instead, Matthew, Jonathan, and Philip mitigated many "meltdowns," led frequent hikes to the duck pond, organized Dance Revolution contests, triaged skinned knees and broken bones, and shared their ping-pong skills and their pets. I never once heard them complain or act like we somehow owed them a thing.

My children (Riley and Wolfie—now grown) love the Talamini boys (now the Talamini men), not just because they were faithful servants, but because the Talamini boys cared enough to spend the time and effort to get to know them. Perhaps their empathic nature was rooted in the memory of what it's like to be a vulnerable, impressionable child. They became familiar teacher-friends who were valued, admired, and respected by the dozen or so young house-church children whom they watched and served. I wonder if the Talaminis ever realized the strong positive impact they had on our children and how much they blessed *our* lives. Do *you* ever consider the impact *your* godly influence may have on the lives of your students and their families?

During my own teaching career, I have not always cleared the Talamini-boy bar.

"Just great," I thought, as LaQuita retched for the third day running. The acrid odor of yesterday's accident still lingered over the garbage can. "If the girl is sick, she should stay home!"

Now, the entire lesson is lost. The other students will complain for the rest of class—and they'll gag, some for real and some faking it. I had done a lot of planning and prepping for this lab—how dare she ruin it! Usually, I would try to comfort a sick student, patting his or her back and quietly releasing the student to the nurse. This time, however, I grudgingly wrote LaQuita's pass, yanked the odiferous garbage can into the hallway, and held my breath as I picked up stray remnants with piles of that not-very-absorbent brown paper towel that is science classroom standard issue.

Without gathering her belongings, and with a white tissue thrust against her mouth, LaQuita sashayed out of the room. Most students would be horrified to be the center of such a spectacle, yet she left looking almost proud.

"What is wrong with that child?" I mumbled more to myself than to anyone else in the classroom. "You would think she would stay home until she feels better. At least until she can control her bodily fluids!"

"Oh, she won't be feeling better for another nine months," LaQuita's best friend, Chantel, quipped. "And she's not the only one, either. My two best friends are pregnant, and they're both in my math class. You think this room smells bad; you should check out math class!"

Can you imagine how I felt at this point? I was devastated about LaQuita's predicament, concerned about Chantel, feeling sorry for my friend the math teacher, and stunned by my new-found knowledge. Here I am, a biology teacher, and I didn't put two and two together—how embarrassing!

As I thought back to LaQuita's recent absences, expanding girth, and deteriorating attitude, everything suddenly made sense. I felt naïve and shamed by my behavior and my judgmental words. I had added to this girl's misery simply because I was annoyed and inconvenienced. I remembered how it felt to be pregnant but still couldn't fathom the conditions LaQuita encountered as such a young mom-to-be. Clearly, I had much more to learn about my students and the environments in which many of them struggle daily for survival.

An hour or so later, LaQuita interrupted my next class, stopping by to pick up her backpack and books. I stopped my instruction long enough to whisper a quiet, "Hope you feel better" and "See you tomorrow?"

Thomas Aquinas's words cut to the quick: "I would rather feel compassion than know the meaning of it." The English word *empathy* is derived from the Greek work *empatheia*, meaning "affection" or "passion." Merriam-Webster defines *empathy* as "the action of understanding, being aware of, being sensitive to, and vicariously experiencing the feelings, thoughts, and experience of another."

What good is empathy, prayer, or meditation if it only generates emotions—if our empathy, prayers, or meditation don't lead us to action? The Dalai Lama once said, "It is not enough just to meditate and pray, which are always good things to do, but we also must take positive action in this world."

When I fail to pass on Christ's love through actions of kindness and compassion, I am hoarding his greatest gift. If a photo of a starving child moves me, yet I fail to dash off a check to the agency that can feed him, what good is the emotion? If I care about LaQuita but am quick to dismiss her, my feelings are useless. And if I'm angered by the ignorance surrounding me but fail to open minds to truth, I am not a great teacher!

## Learning from Jesus

Although the word *empathy* doesn't show up in English translations of the Gospels, Jesus consistently showed evidence of compassion and empathy through his words and actions. The Incarnation itself was an act of God's empathy with humanity, allowing Jesus to share fully in the human experience. Throughout his life and ministry, Jesus was committed to helping the helpless and taught his disciples to do likewise. Jesus' parable about the good Samaritan taught this lesson using word pictures, and his miracles modeled it. When two pesky blind men followed Jesus (how did they do that?), he asked what they wanted and had mercy on them (Matthew 9:27-30). In another instance, Jesus told a paralyzed man, "Take heart, son, your sins are forgiven," and the man stood and went home (Matthew 9:2,7).

During a border crossing between Samaria and Galilee, Jesus encountered ten lepers who were feared because of their highly communicable disease. These men, consigned by law to live in the caves outside of town, asked for his help: They "called out in a loud voice, 'Jesus, Master, have pity on us!'" (Luke 17:11-13). Do you suppose that the disciples urged Jesus to continue onward, maybe even objecting to this dangerous detour?

"You know, Jesus, we're already late for our next meeting, and we still have to walk to Jerusalem. This leprosy stuff is risky business—we're on an important teaching tour!" might have easily escaped my lips. Instead of quickening his pace or avoiding eye contact, however, Jesus stopped to help the men.

Mark 8 describes a situation in which Jesus' empathy for a large crowd moves him to miraculous action. Jesus tells his disciples, "I have compassion for these people; they have already been with me three days and have nothing to eat. If I send them home hungry, they will collapse on the way, because some of them have come a long distance" (Mark 8:2-3). Instead of merely empathizing with his hungry students, Jesus miraculously fed more than four thousand that day. He used only a few fish and seven rolls of bread.

In reviewing this account, one has to wonder how Jesus managed to develop empathy or compassion for a crowd. And I can't help but wonder how physically and emotionally exhausting it must have been, even for the Son of God, to feel compassion for so many.

No doubt, Jesus could empathize with crowds because he supernaturally identified with the individuals composing the group. Jesus also understood the conditions of their souls and the issues of their neighborhoods. Could he possibly see beyond the crowd and feel into the hearts of all those who made up the crowd? Clearly, the empathy Jesus felt for the crowd enabled him to teach effectively.

It appears that Jesus' empathy drove him to perform miracles—miracles that displayed God's power, love, and compassion. For instance, a distraught father once brought his convulsing, apparently demon-possessed son to Jesus. "If you can do anything, take pity on us and help us," the father begged. *"If you can?"* Jesus repeated incredulously, before healing the boy (Mark 9:17-29). Another time, a man with leprosy begged to be made clean. Filled with compassion, Jesus "reached out his hand and touched the man. 'I am willing,' he said. 'Be clean!'" (Mark 1:40-41). That is the efficacy of empathy—it can drive us to help others with whatever power or resources we possess.

## Trying What Jesus Taught

"But isn't it miracle enough that I go back into my classroom each day?" you may ask. How right you are! In the words of St. Francis of Assisi, "Start by doing what's necessary, then do what's possible, and suddenly you are doing the impossible." Although we can't reciprocate God's sacrifice for us, we can pass along his love. Jesus even promised that when we help someone else or show someone kindness, Jesus sees our kindness as an act done specifically for him (Matthew 10:40).

Only two days after a stranger had jumped my car battery in the school parking lot, I had the chance to do the same for someone else. I was exhausted from a long day and still needed to do some planning. The next day I would introduce a genetics unit to my biology classes, and I needed to come up with a lesson introduction. It was a wintry western afternoon—the snow that had fallen during the morning was not yet melted, and at five in the afternoon the early setting sun left a stretch of pink atop the mountains. Keys in hand, I hopped out of my truck to grab the mail from our condo mailbox. I opened the box right before his shadow fell over me. I looked up and into the eyes of the tallest, blackest man I'd ever seen in Denver.

"Can you help me, miss?" the man almost whispered. "I am gone for a long time from this country and come back to find vehicle not starting." He reached out for my hand and introduced himself, but whether it was due to his accent or my disorienta-tion, I didn't catch his name.

"No problem," I replied. "I have some jumper cables in the back of my truck. Where's your vehicle?" When he explained that his car was in his garage, I instantly felt a measure of uncertainly. I knew I shouldn't enter a stranger's garage. "You come to garage to help me, yes?"

There was something familiar about this man, and I'd already agreed to help him, so I drove a few hundred feet to his garage door. I tried to explain tactfully that I would help him as long as he left the garage door open. He agreed. Although he knew noth-ing about jump-starting a car, thanks to my own recent rescue, I did: black to black, red to red.

Turns out my lanky, large neighbor knew a lot about jumping of another kind—basketball. Soon after his truck engine turned over, the garage filled with several more gregarious, gracious giants. "Thanks for helping our teammate. We appreciate the favor. Our friend, Dikembe, needs to get to practice, and we need to leave NOW!" Three members of the Denver Nuggets introduced themselves, vigorously pumping my hand while thanking me profusely. Then, they piled into their SUV, like a circus car filling with too many arms and legs, and were gone.

I had found my genetics opening (and Dikembe's address, which, for the record, I did not share). "Why do you suppose that, compared with the rest of us, basketball players are so tall?" I asked my biology students the next day. "Do I have a story to tell you!"

My rare meet-the-Denver-Nuggets-while-you-act-on-empathy scenario left me feeling energized and excited. But more often, when we try to emulate Jesus in our lives, our efforts to help others leave us fatigued.

Once news of his miracles had spread, everybody wanted a piece of Jesus—his time, his touch, his energy. Do you ever feel that way? Matthew 9:36 says, "When he saw the crowds, he had compassion on them, because they were harassed and helpless, like sheep without a shepherd." When he was finished teaching, Jesus dismissed the crowd and sent his disciples away to a quiet mountaintop, where he planned to join them soon. Do you think they went away for a secret planning meeting or because they were exhausted?

Have you ever felt that the demands or needs of others leave you feeling as if you are sucked dry? I've heard more than one teacher describe how at the end of the school day, they felt as if "someone drew the life energy out of me with a huge syringe." Interestingly, after his miraculous feeding of the four thousand, Jesus not only sent the crowd homeward but also withdrew to a restful place (Mark 8:9-10). Empathy, supernatural love, and shared experiences connected Jesus with his students. You have access to the same tools and can use them to relate to your students. When students feel connected to their teacher, they are more apt to listen and learn. Receptive students reward their teachers by learning their lessons well. Can you see the happy circle of education that we have going when we make the effort toward empathy?

It is important to remember that as we teach and serve others, we are directly serving Christ. "The King will reply, 'Truly I tell you, whatever you did for one of the least of these brothers and sisters of mine, you did for me'" (Matthew 25:40). Your compassion for that dirty, smart-mouthed kid is mercy shown to Jesus. The time spent after class with the slow learner is time given directly to Jesus. Lunchtime shared with the disheveled, hungry, pregnant girl is a meal shared with Jesus. In gladly serving and empathizing with those he has sent, you serve the risen Lord!

## P.S. (PRACTICAL SUGGESTIONS)

Sandwich tough messages between soft words. If you have to tell a student bad news (you're failing my class, your behavior must be punished), tell him or her something good before and after. This is not just softening the blow but is biblically based consideration founded on empathy. In Revelation, John compliments each church before and after telling its members the problems they must address—and John's words are direct revelations from Jesus Christ.

Pray for your most annoying student(s). Wouldn't you want them to do the same for you?

Use your imagination to explore how some of your students live. Think about the problems and challenges they meet daily. Then, talk to them—listen carefully when they share their issues, concerns, and life stories.

Share a meal with a student. Put aside one lunch break to eat and meet (an "eating meeting"). Ask questions, share food, and listen.

Ask God to give you a caring heart toward your students, expecting that the Lord will teach you more than you might want to know.

Read and study the Gospel of Matthew. Notice the many instances in which Jesus shows empathy to his students and his friends.

Notice someone today—keep your eyes, ears, and heart open to someone who might otherwise go throughout his or her day unnoticed. Is there a student who is lost in the crowd but in dire need of attention? Even a thimbleful of positive attention can brighten a young person's world.

Remain alert and mindful of your own needs. Find ways to relax and energize, especially when the students you serve drain you of your energy.

God loves us so much that he calls us his children (1 John 3:1). Thank God for loving you as a Father loves his own and ask for the Spirit's help in loving his children whom you teach and serve.

If you aren't already a part of a fellowship or study group, find like-minded adults who can support you in your quest to teach like Jesus. In the same way that your students need compassion, *you* need to feel support and empathy. Bounce off each other the frustrations, challenges, and joys of the job. Perhaps as you study this book together with them, you will be able to encourage one another.

Unless you remain in the joy of the Lord, you won't have any joy to pass along to your students. Worship, sing, study Scripture, and ask God to fill you with peace, joy, and empathy.

## STUDY GUIDE FOR LESSON 2:
### THE EFFICACY OF EMPATHY

**1.** Can you remember how it felt when you were the age of the students you now teach? What were your greatest concerns? Your greatest fears? Your greatest achievements or joys?

**2.** Read Mark 9:17-29. Why did Jesus respond as he did to this father? In what tone of voice do you suppose Jesus answered, "If you can?" Do you think Jesus was angry? Explain.

**3.** Cite an example of a situation in which you experienced evidence and a positive consequence of the what-goes-around-comes-around phenomenon. How about an example of a negative consequence of the phenomenon? Do you think this phenomenon is a biblical principle or just fodder for chain e-mails? Why?

**4.** Is it enough to feel empathy, or must we follow through on the emotion with action? Search the Scriptures for evidence that supports your response.

**5.** Conversely, is it enough to do good works, or must we strive to feel a certain way (empathy), too? Search the Scriptures for evidence that supports your response.

**6.** Which practical suggestion(s) are you ready to try?

**7.** In what ways might the group with whom you are studying this lesson (if applicable) hold the potential to help you do this?

**8.** What is your specific plan for engaging your chosen practical suggestions?

# THE
# Acknowledgment
## OF
# Audience

**Scripture Lesson:**
John 1:35-50
John 10:1-18
John 14:1-14

*"The only reason I always try to meet and know the parents better is because it helps me to forgive their children." —Louis Johannot*

A brilliant linguist-turned-Wycliffe Bible-translator became a missionary in the highlands of New Guinea. His life was spared by those he came to serve. Imagine the scene of his jeep rumbling along a bumpy jungle road. The thick vegetation that hung over the rutted road of dried mud finally opened to the pink dusk of a jungle sky. Fiery arrows pierced the rapidly darkening sky. An open field, split by the rugged road, was the gathering site for warriors from two neighboring tribes. Faces decorated in war paint sported decorative bone piercings. Weapons were raised, and war whoops filled the night air. The missionary and his American visitor (now crouched on the floor of the jeep, quaking in fear) continued moving toward the battlefield. The quivering guest supposed that his mind was playing tricks on him—the expectation of a wild country, fatigue from an extensive transcontinental trip, maybe even the inhalation of so much road dust may have spurred his imagination. But no, the scene was all too real.

Moonlight revealed two factions reloading their bows as the jeep approached. Strangely, for just a few moments, the warriors paused. Scantily clad, wire-muscled soldiers from both sides of the dusty jungle road lowered their weapons and turned toward the jeep. They waved respectfully and warmly greeted the missionary by name. The missionary waved back and returned greetings before speeding away with a lead foot and heavy heart. Warriors from both tribes were his friends, yet they were bent on killing each other—the men he had spent a lifetime learning to love.

The warring tribes did not attempt to know each other personally, the way they knew the missionary, so they were determined to kill each other. *To know me is to love me. . . .* You've heard the saying, which at first seems egotistical. But think about it: if you don't know me, how *can* you love me? And the reverse is at least partially true. If you don't love me, you probably won't endeavor to know me, either.

## Learning from Jesus

Jesus came from another world, another realm altogether. He came to Earth with a superhuman ability to know and to love us. And yet, perhaps in order to truly understand the human experience, our God came to Earth as a baby who needed his diaper changed, his wounds tended, and his meals prepared. Jesus grew up in a backwater village as a working-class mortal who felt hunger, fatigue, temptation, and pain. He experienced what it is to be human during his thirty-three years on our planet. While here, he reached out to his audience and spoke in a manner that they could understand—When he was teaching in the synagogue, he referenced the Hebrew prophets. When addressing the farmers and shepherds, he spoke using agricultural metaphors and parables to which his agrarian audience could relate. In John's Gospel, Jesus describes himself in a way that his livestock farming audience understands: "I am the good shepherd," he says. "I know my sheep and my sheep know me—just as the Father knows me and I know the Father—and I lay down my life for the sheep" (John 10:14-15). Jesus acknowledged his audience; he understood and loved them.

Judas betrayed Jesus for thirty pieces of silver (Matthew 26:15). Raised in a spiritually rich family and trained as a carpenter, Jesus understood all too well the social, political, and economic issues surrounding him. Do you suppose that Jesus spent so much time with people in order to better understand *them* or so that they could know *him*?

After Jesus taught in the temple courts, the Jews were amazed and asked, "How did this man get such learning without having been taught?" (John 7:14-15). Because Jesus proclaimed himself as God, we assume he didn't have to study the Torah, which he had written. But who is to say that in human form Jesus didn't study? Along with carpentry, Jesus examined the behaviors and attitudes of the town bullies and the sanctimonious temple scholars. Jesus knew the buzz of the land and was familiar with the knowledge base of his audience. Jesus knew that, in order to explain another realm to his students, he had to reference concepts that his audience found familiar.

Is it surprising that one of the Greek words for "to know" also means "to love"? Notice the symmetry between knowing and loving. If we really know people, we can love them. And they can sense when we really care.

## Trying What Jesus Taught

Missionaries often invest years, even decades, learning to appreciate and understand the people they serve. They might spend more time getting to know their audience than they do teaching, preaching, or sharing God's Word. Teachers, like missionaries, often find themselves in foreign territory. I know I did.

My experience as an instructor in a predominantly middle- to upper-middle-class high school in suburban New Jersey prepared me to teach students with backgrounds like my own. It was hard work, but I fit in. It was a comfortable place—the kind of school I attended.

I recall telling my suburban teaching colleagues that I expected to spend my career teaching in New Jersey and promised them that if I ever left our school, I certainly had no intentions of ever working in the inner city. What an arrogant statement and prescient mistake! Very soon after saying this, I got married and moved across the country, following my new husband to where he would attend medical school in Colorado.

The job market at that time was tight, so I took the first job I was offered—a lab tech job at the National Jewish Hospital. On the fourth day of work, the phone rang. Would I take an interview with the local public-school system? Only if they could finish the meeting before I was due at the hospital. Say around 6:30 a.m.? They agreed.

The following Monday, just two days after my apparently successful interview, I walked into foreign territory. Instead of my familiar suburban high school, I found myself in a strange land. Believe me when I tell you that upon entering *any* high school, adults experience confusion, possible flashbacks, and certain culture shock. When I walked into Midway High School that morning, I was suddenly immersed in a swirl of unknown cultures. I found myself in a place where gangs, weapons, drugs, and teen pregnancy were common concerns—where parole officers became familiar, and where I was the first white female science teacher in some time.

I found holes in the drywall behind my classroom desk and looked down to find bullet casings scattered on the frayed, dirty carpet. When I frantically showed the casings to my new Department Chair, he comforted me with, "They're just from a .22. They won't hurt you!" I knew then I was truly out of my element, out on a limb, maybe out of my mind. I believed that God wanted me in the classroom, bullet holes and all—but I felt lost, oh so lost!

The following Sunday I was leaving the sanctuary after the morning worship service when a proper little church lady approached me, asking: "Dahling, what do you DOOOO?"

"I'm a schoolteacher," I replied.

"Wonderful! And where, I wonder, do you teach?"

Excited by her interest, I replied, "I teach science at Midway High."

Then she countered, "A public school? What a shame! I say, have you considered the mission field?"

I was so angry and stunned that I couldn't respond. Yet my conversation with that church lady opened my mind to a novel concept: I was working in what felt like foreign territory, and I *was* on a mission! The school where I taught was as alien to me as any mission field I could imagine. From that day on, I started to view my job as more than a paycheck—I began seeing my job as my mission.

Despite this epiphany, I was still the white woman out of her element. Many nights I cried myself to sleep—not just because of my exhaustion and loneliness, but because of the overwhelming violence, poverty, and dysfunction I witnessed daily. I relied on God's protection and the promise that with the Spirit's empowerment, I could make a difference. Along with the help of colleagues and students. I quickly realized that *I* needed an education—I had to learn more about the community and my students or I would lose heart, never truly caring about them.

So, I decided to check out the Goodwill store in my school's neighborhood. I had overheard a few girls describing its location while quietly comparing their respective finds. I could think of no better way to learn the lay of the land and go green in my clothing purchases.

I arrived at Goodwill, not too far from school, and found the demographics of the folks loitering outside the store not much different from Midway's population. In other words, I was the minority, once again—and that was okay.

Once inside, I found a nicely organized and sufficiently stocked superstore. Several men's suits caught my eye. As I walked over to the suit rack, I glanced up to see a familiar face that quickly disappeared behind a rack of clothes. Curious, I stared for a long moment in the direction where I thought I'd seen someone I knew. Eventually Maria, one of my current students, stepped out from behind the rack. She seemed skittish, like a startled deer, and was clearly embarrassed about something.

"What's up, Maria?" I cheerfully greeted her. "Find any bargains?" Maria looked confused and alarmed. She took in the sight of me, already loaded down with multiple clothes draped over my arms. Maria looked at the suits, looked at me, and then back at my finds before dropping her eyes.

"You shop here, too?" Maria asked shyly.

"This is my first time at this particular store, but I shop 'used' all the time. I love the suits they sell *and* the prices. I've learned to convert the men's pants to long women's skirts. They're perfect for the classroom. I get my ties in these places, too. How about you—do you come here often?"

"Once in a while," Maria responded.

I stepped a bit closer and whispered, "Well, this is our little secret. We don't want to let everyone know what great deals we can get here, right?" She looked relieved before we parted ways.

I realized Maria had been embarrassed to be seen shopping in the Goodwill superstore—perhaps this was the only place she could afford to buy her clothing. Besides scoring two sweet new suits, this trip sensitized me to the limited finances available to many of my students.

The more I learn about my students, the more I appreciate their efforts to rise above the often-difficult situations in which they live. Sure, I don't know firsthand what it's like to sleep every night with two sisters on one tiny mattress. I haven't felt the pangs of an empty stomach that isn't filled because my mom's boyfriend ate the last frozen burrito. I haven't experienced the claws of fear as the National Immigration Service breaks down the hotel door—again. And I never once waited an entire night in the emergency room to see if the bullet could be removed from my brother's shoulder or tried to finish my homework in the police station where my mom sat in a holding pen.

Yet, as I listen to another student describe her latest challenge, I try to comprehend what it all means. As I listen, I learn about another world—a world far different from the one I have always known. In the same way that missionaries study their message *and* the people they will serve, I need to understand and appreciate my students before I can effectively teach them or love them.

## A Kind of Commencement Address

The culmination of my nine years at Midway H.S. was celebrated at their end-of-year senior farewell assembly. Tears streamed so profusely from my eyeglass-covered eyes that it wasn't even worth wiping them away from my face with the backs of my sweaty hands. I stood in the middle of the gym while sixteen hundred or so students stared down from the bleachers, strangely silent. Like the graduating senior class, the teachers with whom I huddled in the middle of the gym floor were also leaving. Our school's high transiency rate was not limited to its student body—the faculty turned over frequently, too. After years of wanting to leave Midway, I finally understood my mission and wanted to stay, but my husband's medical internship match at John's Hopkins Hospital mandated a cross-country move and a major life change for me. The farewell assembly had been tweaked to include our own mini-teacher farewell event. The assembly organizer had asked each of the exiting staff members to write a short statement that would be read to the student body. After announcing our names and our teaching assignments, the announcer would read our prewritten summaries, which, we were strictly instructed, must each include a report of our greatest accomplishment at Midway High School.

So, about a week before the farewell event, I pondered: What *was* my greatest accomplishment here? Should I list the teaching awards I received—and was the Colorado Outstanding Biology Teacher Award more meaningful than the award from the American Heart Association? Should I mention my recent fellowship appointments or the credits I'd accrued since landing here almost nine years ago? I pulled out my updated résumé, puzzling as to which parts really mattered. What mattered to the students in that gym? What really mattered to me? After a few moments of contemplation, the answer was clear. It seemed hokey when I wrote it but sounded right when the announcer read my state-ment: "During my time at Midway, I have been honored to work with some of the finest minds in the country. And in working with so many fine students, I have come to love them."

How much is it worth to get to know your students—not just to learn their names (although that alone may be a daunting task) but to really explore who they are: What excites them, what music do they listen to, and what do they do after school? A small invest-ment in this department might well lead to better classroom dis-cussions, more effective teaching, and better lesson planning. To get to know your student audience, you don't need to invest huge amounts of money or all your time. You can get to know your students by talking to them and (more importantly) by listening to them. Your students probably spend more of their waking hours in school than anywhere else, and because you are there with them, you can potentially learn much more than you ever thought you would know. If you listen to your students, you will come to know them, and in knowing them you will learn to love them, too.

## P.S. (PRACTICAL SUGGESTIONS)

Make a strong and early effort to learn all of your students' names. You can start by setting up a seating chart (that can later be abandoned, if you choose). Keep the chart on a clipboard in front of you. During that first week, call on your students by name, indicating that you already recognize and know them.

On the first day with your students, ask them to complete a brief personal survey. Ask students to supply name and address, contact information, career goal, special interests, hobbies, or sports, favor-ite class, expectations for your class, and questions they might have about you or your course. Correlate the survey responses with your seating chart. File cards or questionnaires for future reference.

Jump-start conversations with your students using informa-tion gleaned from those index cards or questionnaires. Perhaps you will find that you share interests with them.

Ask a trusted student or two how you might most effectively become better acquainted with their neighborhood.

Find a copy of the most recent school yearbook, or if you are teaching in the church setting, secure a copy of the church photo directory. Study the names and faces of those students who are in your class group.

Ask students to tell you the name of their favorite music artist or song title(s). Listen to the same music (in small doses, perhaps) during your off time.

Find out which foods and restaurants your students enjoy. Order the same takeout, or visit one of their favorite restaurants for a quick snack after school. Consider an outing for lunch or dinner. You might discover a great new place to eat.

Visit the closest mall or other popular destination near your school. Note the surroundings (so you can report on your adventures to your students later) and be alert to groups of teens who might include your students. If you see any of your students, greet them cheerfully.

Ask students where they shop for clothing and shoes or where they work. Visit one or more of these establishments—no need to buy a thing.

Attend a sports game or event hosted by your school or community. Find out beforehand which of your students might be involved. Be sure to congratulate participants on their performance or competition the next time you see them.

Consider attending public events to which students invite you. Graduation parties are often good venues for observing student lifestyles and learning more about your community. Plays or musical performances often showcase students' talents that are otherwise hidden.

Ask God to give you a spirit of curiosity and concern regarding your students. Pray that a positive attitude will show through your face, your actions, and your words.

Pray for your students, realizing that you may be the only person in the whole world praying for any one of them.

## STUDY GUIDE FOR LESSON 3:
## THE ACKNOWLEDGMENT OF AUDIENCE

**1.** Think of a time when you were able to avoid trouble because you knew someone who could alter or influence a potentially bad situation. Describe the scenario and circumstances.

**2.** Recall a time when you were able to positively influence a potentially bad situation and help someone who knew you. Describe that scenario and circumstances.

**3.** How do you feel when you enter "foreign" territory (e.g., a context where you are a racial, gender, or other minority; a social situation where you know no one; an unfamiliar neighborhood)? In such a situation, how could someone else make you feel more comfortable?

**4.** How could your answers to the questions posed above translate to your classroom or to the students whom you teach? In other words, what could you do to help new students feel more comfortable in the classroom context?

**5.** Text in this chapter reads, "Jesus came from another world, another realm altogether. He came to earth with a super-human ability to know and to love us." Why does the author describe Jesus' ability to know us as superhuman?

**6.** See John 14:1-14. What does Jesus promise his followers? Do you believe that these promises extend to all followers? Why or why not?

**7.** According to John 14, how does Jesus intend to compensate for our human limitations?

**8.** Which practical suggestion(s) are you willing to embrace this week?

# THE
# Strength
## OF A
# Story

**Scripture Lesson:**
Matthew 13:1-17
Mark 4:33-34
Luke 8:4-18

*"What the teacher is, is more important than what he [or she] teaches."* —Karl Menninger

"Did I ever tell you about the rainy night in the Midwest when I slept in a field with a friend and a whole bunch of cows? Do you know what it's like to wake up with a strange cow all up in your face—and then to realize that it's not a dream?" A few students moved toward the tables at the front of the room, where up until that moment, I had stood helplessly in horror watching the activities of shop class gone substitute-teacher-bad. Nails were still scattered on the floor, but at least the sawdust was settling. The scent of fresh-cut wood filling the air was somewhat pleasant, reminding me of something comforting from childhood. But I also smelled danger.

I desperately spun my tale, praying that the rest of the students would be interested enough to join our impromptu story time. I hoped they might turn off their circular saws and stop throwing pieces of 2 x 4 across the room. The airborne wood chunks did pose a true safety threat, so I had no intention of teaching a single thing. Besides, at the time I had no knowledge of power tools or woodworking. Yet I didn't want my first day substitute teaching in woodshop to be associated with maiming mayhem—if a student lost a limb, it wouldn't look good on my résumé. This experience made my day subbing in home economics (with the flying pie dough) look like a romp in the park.

One travel story followed another until the potentially dangerous 45 minutes of shop class were complete. As the bell sounded, I silently thanked the Lord for his protection, for the adventures of my life, and for the stories the Spirit had given me. I was astounded by the power a few stories wielded—they distracted and calmed the students in my care who could have maimed me or each other.

The tales I told that day were neither instructive nor planned—they were recited on the spur of the moment and were a desperate grasp at classroom control. They allowed me to survive what turned out to be my first and, blessedly, last day substituting for the Intro to Woodworking teacher. Imagine how powerful your stories could be if they related to the subject matter and were part of your lesson plan!

Like your life, my life is made up of one story after another. If only I could gain the perspective that would allow me to see life's annoying, seemingly negative experiences as opportunities to gather a good story. While teaching in a rough urban high school, my frustration and angst reached dangerous levels. I was far from home, my medical student husband was studying hard and mostly unavailable, and my medical benefits didn't cover therapy. So I vented my frustrations, recounting the day's events, into a tape recorder. The activity was a form of therapy, and the stories I recorded later became the vignettes in a devotional book, *Morning Meetings with Jesus: 180 Devotions for Teachers*. My stories did have some usefulness, after all.

## Learning from Jesus

We might picture history's great teachers as dry philosophers with nary an interesting tale. Yet written records show quite a different picture: The Socratic method involved role-playing, purposeful questioning, and a good amount of storytelling. Plato spun many a tale and wrote myths that he believed helped in teaching difficult and elusive concepts. Chinese scholars point out that most of Confucius's teaching did not rely on deductive reasoning but instead used analogies and clichés to explain his ideas.

Jesus was a master storyteller who knew the importance of not leaving any child behind long before federal governments adopted the concept. And he used stories to do so. Stories addressed the needs of his visual and auditory learners. He employed familiar and vivid images: a light under a bushel basket, a lost lamb found, a woman frantically searching for a lost coin.

Jesus, the master Teacher, taught using parables that featured situations and characters that his audience could understand. For example, in the story of the prodigal son, all people, regardless of their stations in life, could see themselves in at least one of the story's players. Jesus' stories were realistic and confronted issues his listeners encountered. His stories replaced lecture or preaching and taught more effectively than either. For at least one audience, Jesus concentrated on the parable method: The Gospel writer tells us that "Jesus spoke all these things to the crowd in parables; he did not say anything to them without using a parable" (Matthew 13:34).

Whether tailoring his lessons to a small group or addressing the masses, Jesus chose stories that resonated. When speaking with the scholarly Pharisees, Jesus catered to their academic backgrounds by referencing and quoting Hebrew Scriptures with which they were familiar. For example, in Matthew 12, Jesus discussed references to King David that his Jewish audience would have known by heart.

However, when teaching a crowd made up largely of farmers and laborers in a country setting, Jesus rarely discussed the intricate academics of Scripture but instead spoke of soil and planting techniques. In a time and place where the best parties were those associated with weddings, Jesus compared the bride with the church and the bridegroom with himself (Matthew 9:15).

The Gospel accounts of Matthew, Mark, and Luke recount at least forty stories that Jesus used in his teaching. These stories could be classified as parables, metaphors, similes, or word pictures. Regardless of what you call them, Jesus' stories conveyed such powerful lessons that, thousands of years later, we still can learn from them:

Matthew 13:1-23, the parable of the sower
Matthew 13:31-32, the parable of the mustard seed
Matthew 22:1-14, the parable of the wedding banquet
Luke 15:1-10, the parables of the lost sheep and the lost coin
Luke 15:11-32, the parable of the lost (prodigal) son
Luke 16:1-15, the parable of the shrewd manager

New followers of Christ are often advised by more mature believers to study the Bible, starting with the New Testament. The first book of the New Testament consists of one story after another. Check it out for yourself—the Gospel of Matthew is one nonstop collection of stories. This accounting shows us a Jesus who wasn't trying to entertain or act like the star of a show. Rather, we see a patient teacher using stories to make a point, to connect with his audience, and to focus their minds and hearts on concepts of the heavenly realm.

## Trying What Jesus Taught

Teachers can effectively employ the strength of stories collected from others: accounts we've read, Jesus' parables, or tales borrowed from friends. At some point, however, it's time to gather our own unique repertoire. Before approaching this task, take warning: God is not only the omnipotent ruler of the universe but is also the Master of Humor. God's storyline for each of us is likely infused with frighteningly amusing events.

Suffice it to say that I often miss God's humor and fail to appreciate the process that leads to a great story, focusing instead on my frustration or discomfort. It is sometimes easier to gather and perfect the telling of your own stories years after the experiences. Perhaps this is because it can take a while to recover from some of the story-gathering incidents. Like my recent mascot experience.

Some people say that they do volunteer work for the PTA. They mention committee work, successful fundraisers, or their membership program. I'm involved with that stuff too, yet it's another topic that gets me going. You won't quite understand the importance of the recovery process previously mentioned until you know about Rodger.

When the Spirit Committee ordered the foam head for our new mascot, Rodger the Colt, we decided to save a few bucks by ordering a head without the air circulation fan. Turns out this was a poor decision—we now know that virtually all the professional teams order mascot heads with the air flow fan, so that the person under the costume can breathe. Small detail—until it's *you* under that head!

The committee also wanted an attractive horse head that would not show evidence of human eyes. Were we delusional enough to think that the students wouldn't suspect that there was a human inside? Nevertheless, our large foam head was delivered minus eye-holes, and was later "doctored" by the committee chair to include mere slits positioned near the colt's nostrils. This meant that the person under the mascot head would be essentially blind and in need of a sighted human guide to direct his or her movements. The committee planned to formally introduce their new investment during the halftime of the annual February physical education fundraiser, a popular staff-versus-student basketball game, traditionally played in the gym of the local high school.

Wearing the full-body horse costume, complete with hoof-slipper feet and the huge foam head, I stood anxiously in the wings waiting. My thick, polyester-backed, hairy costume was garbed in a specially made 4X-sized T-shirt, and I felt the sweat running down into the hoof slippers. Even outside the nearly full gymnasium, the heat and humidity rapidly approached Baltimore-in-August levels. In one hoof, I held a red and white shaker pompom, and with the other front hoof, I planned to wildly wave to my soon-to-be-adoring crowd. No, this was not like the

*I Love Lucy* episode; I wore the entire horse costume, not just its hindquarters.

Finally, it was halftime. There was a drumroll before the announcer called Rodger the Colt out to the middle of the gym. To get there, Rodger had to blindly crash through a large paper banner—and soon all eyes were on the horse! Rodger's debut started out fine—he pawed the floor, danced, wiggled, and wildly waved to the crowd as the announcer introduced the new mascot. Ah, the glory of it all.

An unexpected throng of students suddenly swarmed the gym floor, grabbing my hands, my torso, and my tail (I mean *Rodger's* hands, torso, and tail). The oxygen deprivation and limited field of view probably protected me from full-out panic as hundreds of students came for a piece of Rodger. The crowd closed in like European fans swarming the field after a World Cup win.

I lost contact with my human guide, who up until then had miraculously moved me forward, and I felt myself falling. Strangely, my back end didn't hit the floor, and although I wasn't moving one foot in front of the other, I somehow rolled away from the crowd. Sensing the desperate nature of the situation, my guide (the gym teacher), had pushed me into a wheelchair and rolled me out of the limelight and away from the crazed crowd. Where the wheelchair came from I still don't know. When I say that I'm indebted to the staff of my children's elementary school, it's no understatement. I suppose the moral to this story is that, in much the same way, we are all indebted to God's Spirit who protects and encourages us as we build our story cache and who inspires us to use the appropriate stories to engage, instruct, and motivate our students.

# P.S. (PRACTICAL SUGGESTIONS)

Practice storytelling outside of your classroom. Tell a child a bedtime story, or regale your spouse or a friend with a dinnertime story related to the events of your day. Experiment with sharing your experiences in an engaging, entertaining manner.

You know how dying people report that their lives pass before their eyes? Why not reflect sooner? Think back over your relationships, experiences (inside and outside of a classroom), adventures, and activities. Consider reviewing the past year or two—allowing your mind to discover your potential story-stash.

At the end of one teaching day, decide on the funniest or most memorable event of your day. Even if you haven't quite recovered from the incident, record the details and describe the event in story form. This can be a cathartic and healing process, kind of like a form of therapy. Consider keeping a daily or weekly record of your similar stories; besides giving you a chance to vent each day, the written journal or audio recording might later serve as a source of comic relief or encouragement.

Read the Gospel account as recorded by Matthew. The book can be read in one sitting or during several study sessions. Notice how Jesus used stories, parables, and metaphors throughout his ministry to teach his students.

Identify one story that you have successfully used in your teaching. Try to figure out why that particular story helped you communicate a concept or idea. What aspects of your success story can be incorporated into other teaching stories? Look at your lesson plans for the upcoming week or next several days. Choose one topic that you can supplement using a story (whether it is your own or someone else's). Outline the basic points of your story before using it as part of a lesson. If possible, repeat the same story to more than one class.

In Rick Warren's *The Purpose Driven Life*, the author urges Christians to discover their life stories. He suggests writing down and reciting your story. Warren points out that our stories can become our witness—that people are more likely to listen to our life stories than to a sermon. The strength of *your* story isn't limited to entertaining or teaching academic or curricular concepts to your students—it might be someone's path to redemption!

STUDY GUIDE FOR LESSON 4:
**THE STRENGTH OF A STORY**

**1.** When have you used stories in the same way as the author—as survival tools? Explain what happened.

**2.** Are you comfortable teaching with stories? Why or why not?

**3.** Read Matthew 13–22. Take note of the parables or stories used to describe the kingdom of heaven. Which of the stories most resonates with you? Why?

**4.** Determine and develop your own story. Begin by writing three to five lines that tell the story of why you became a teacher, coach, or leader.

**5.** Why do you think storytellers are revered in so many cultures? In what ways does American culture value (or fail to value) storytelling? Why?

**6.** Do stories teach better when the characters and scenarios are familiar? Why might this be so?

**7.** Which practical suggestion(s) are you ready to try this week?

# THE
# Delight
## OF
# Delegation

**Scripture Lesson:**
Luke 6:12-16
Luke 8:1-3
Luke 10
John 4
Acts 6:1-7

*"When you teach your son, you teach your son's son."* —*The Talmud*

The pounding of my sneakered feet on the bike path, the music blaring through my earphones, and the beauty surrounding me should have wiped away the internal voices that plagued me with each step of my daily run. Usually this would be the perfect way to unwind and forget the worries of the day. Yet the mountains in the distance that showcased the sunset and the crisp, dry air that filled my oxygen-hungry lungs only heightened my awareness of how desperate I had become. I was concurrently bathed in the beauty of nature and the angst of my day.

Did I finish grading that last pile of tests? Where did I put the materials for tomorrow's lab? I'll have to wash up the glassware from today's lab as soon as I get into school tomorrow because only now do I recall being interrupted by a student who needed help while I had been running hot water into the sink. I must remember to leave early tomorrow. Did I send out that house-church e-mail reminder—and which teens are watching the younger children Sunday night? Maybe if I make a simple dinner, I'll have time to type up the handout for tomorrow's lesson and the flyer that I need to send home before the field trip. How will I make two hundred copies of each before classes if I have to finish washing up that glassware?

A prairie dog came out of its burrow and looked at me quizzically. It must have been wondering what was wrong with the slowly lumbering lady with the furrowed brow. The little "dog" looked so cute and unhurried. I had the sudden urge to kick it. Instead, I focused on the path ahead.

I was overwhelmed and anxious—there weren't enough hours in the day. My job was beginning to affect my emotional health. If I couldn't escape my teaching-related worries while running (an activity that usually requires all my emotional and physical energy), I was clearly approaching the edge.

## Learning from Jesus

Although being one with the Father in heaven, Jesus continually prayed, asking God for assistance. Just think of it—Jesus was not afraid to ask for help. He not only relied on God's assistance but also allowed people to help him. We don't find any biblical accounts of Jesus showing concern for the details associated with his group's frequent travel schedule or contacting friends to confirm lodging or meal planning. Is there any record of him organizing fundraisers or bargaining with fig vendors in the marketplace? I didn't think so.

With the future of humanity hanging on Jesus successfully completing his mission, our Lord needed to be an effective manager who was also a discerning delegator. Jesus would have delegated many tasks and responsibilities to those he trusted. And trust is the critical component. Jesus delegated to others the tasks that would have distracted from his mission. To be freed to cure the sick, teach in the temple, and counsel the weary, Jesus needed time. Consequently, some decisions and tasks of life on the road had to fall to others. Are you able to trust others with decisions that will affect your welfare?

Jesus did understand the importance of finding food and shelter for himself and his disciples, and he was not ignorant of money matters. After all, he came from a craftsman's family that relied on fine workmanship and good business dealings. He most likely spent his early years observing the home management skills of his mother and the trade expertise of his father.

The fourth chapter of John's Gospel describes Jesus' encounter with a Samaritan woman at a well. The event marked one of Jesus' most poignant and radical lessons. Perhaps this encounter was so powerful because during this meeting, Jesus crossed multiple cultural and religious barriers. He was alone with a woman, a social faux pas in those days. Why was Jesus alone? We find the answer in verse 8: His disciples had gone into the village to buy some food. Jesus trusted his friends with the grocery shopping and menu planning. We also learn that this woman was a despised Samaritan with an eventful past and an uncertain future, yet Jesus asked *her* for a favor—a drink of water.

Most of us avoid discussing money. It's an uncomfortable, charged topic. But did you ever think about how Jesus funded his ministry? Most likely, he didn't pass an offering basket through the synagogue or circulate his hat for donations. If he did, the proceeds probably would have been confiscated before he left. Jesus was not a beggar! Instead, Luke's record intimates that Jesus accepted monetary contributions from wealthy individuals. We find that Jesus and his mission were largely funded by contributions from women of means. Scripture tells us: "The Twelve were with him, and also some women who had been cured of evil spirits and diseases; Mary (called Magdalene) from whom seven demons had come out; Joanna the wife of Chuza, the manager of Herod's household; Suzanna; and many others. These women were helping to support them out of their own means" (Luke 8:1b-3).

During this time in Israel's history, women did not enjoy the status and privileges of men but were considered to be their husbands' possessions. In this social climate, it was unusual for women to follow Jesus from place to place and even more remarkable that their husbands allowed it.

After reading Luke's succinct accounts, my preconceived notions of Jesus and his band of followers as communicants of a purely "guy thing" melt away. Jesus was, and continues to be, the bearer of Good News meant for everyone. Jesus not only challenged the religious norms but was also a social revolutionary. He welcomed these female supporters, embracing their close association with him and accepting their financial assistance.

Jesus did not have a dysfunctional or controlling nature. "What is it with the fleabag inn you picked this time, John? I trusted you to choose reasonably priced accommodations, and *this* is where you put our money? Clearly, you need more guidance—didn't you even check the *Galilean Guidebook* before you sent our deposit?" No, these are not words we read in any of the Gospel accounts. Jesus was not a control freak.

The fact that Jesus chose human beings to be his interns, companions, and co-missionaries speaks to the importance of delegation and his willingness to practice it. Merriam-Webster's Dictionary defines *delegation* as "the act of empowering to act for another—the *delegation* of responsibilities." Holding all the authority of God, Jesus certainly could have accomplished his mission on his own, yet he chose a group to help him, a select few to whom he would eventually delegate his responsibilities. In Mark's Gospel, we read that Jesus "appointed twelve—designating them apostles—that they might be with him and that he might send them out to preach and to have authority to drive out demons" (3:14-15). Jesus didn't *need* their help, so it seems that he *wanted* to be with them as human beings. Furthermore, Jesus shared with his apostles both his mission *and* his authority. And what a job Jesus did with them—in time, these twelve (and the dozens who joined them) turned the world right-side-up!

However, Jesus did not go overboard with delegating, either. He continued preaching, teaching, healing, and traveling from town to town. Although the Gospels describe a scenario when Jesus napped through a heavy storm at sea, we have no records of Jesus napping while his disciples were teaching or healing the masses. Jesus wasn't a slacker—he worked hard, hiked constantly, rose early, and toiled into the late hours.

While Jesus worked, he modeled to his apostles the tasks that he would eventually delegate to them. Healings and miracles were a focal point of Jesus' three-year ministry—they were a big "draw" for the crowds that followed him from town to town. Yet once Jesus' disciples had witnessed enough of these healings and miracles, Jesus delegated the responsibility for performing miracles to the twelve. Matthew tells us that Jesus instructed his disciples to "heal the sick, raise the dead, cleanse those who have leprosy, drive out demons" (10:8). Can you imagine the shudder of incredulity that rippled through their ranks with this command? Jesus not only instructed his disciples to teach and perform miracles, but he also gave them authority to do both, assuring his understudies that the one "who welcomes you welcomes me, and anyone who welcomes me welcomes the one who sent me" (Matthew 10:40).

## Trying What Jesus Taught

I didn't kick the cute prairie dog on my afternoon run. Neither did I immediately solve my problem of my limited time and overwhelming responsibilities. It wasn't until I felt hopelessly overwhelmed that I sought counsel. I observed that a wise and experienced colleague who taught in the classroom right next door rarely seemed flustered. He managed to balance his teaching and family while managing two part-time businesses. How did he do it? Of course, he was more experienced than I, certainly organized, and popular with his students. I also noticed that this wise teacher accepted help.

I finally consulted with my esteemed colleague and came away with a few valuable suggestions. My colleague advised me to keep my students busy by assigning multiple projects per day, but suggested that I grade only a select few assignments. He told me to carefully choose student assistants and take the time to properly train them. I learned to treat my assistants well, praising and rewarding them often. He told me that "when you give up control, sometimes things don't turn out exactly as you had hoped. Occasionally, mistakes will be made, and you will be inconvenienced. Get over it!"

Throughout the year, I did learn to accept help from two trustworthy student assistants. The time I invested in training these godsent assistants initially seemed wasteful—I couldn't see the return. Why spend thirty minutes setting up an answer sheet that showed every possible test response? How could I come out ahead after investing ten minutes of instruction on how to properly wash and dry a test tube? I could have washed them *all* in that time. And sometimes I counted on a student to prep for a laboratory, only to find the student absent on the day I needed the work done. Eventually I learned which students could be trusted and how to stagger their tasks. I also planned lessons further ahead—if I needed a cart full of supplies for Friday, I would start the setup on Wednesday afternoon instead of Thursday evening. Then, if my helpers were absent on Thursday, it was no big deal.

Over time, the investment was multiplied many-fold. My assistants helped me grade papers and organize labs. They graciously cleaned stinky petri dishes and scoured glassware. Every hour they donated to helping me was one hour that I was free to do something else; sometimes that translated to a better lesson plan, a more creative laboratory activity, or the chance to work one on one with needy students.

However, even with the help of several trusted student assistants, I still couldn't do it all. I learned to accept the help of veteran colleagues—when they offered a ready-made lab exercise, I was quick to accept. When the school hired a photocopy specialist, I swallowed my apprehension (would this person have my class activities copied in time?) and allowed the professional to make almost all of my copies for me. When I was offered a newer, more efficient computer grading program, I snatched it up like a bargain shopper on Black Friday. If Jesus could delegate and accept the support of generous donors, so can I.

# P.S. (PRACTICAL SUGGESTIONS)

Ask colleagues or counselors about recommendations for trustworthy student or parent assistants. (School-related organizations may offer volunteer contact information.) Once you secure a commitment from the volunteer, take the time to train him or her in the desired tasks. Some schools offer community service hours to student assistants; others credit volunteer hours for faith-based service work.

Do you have a list of reliable substitutes you might rely upon when you really need to be absent? If not, ask around—don't be shy about finding connections and securing trustworthy contacts. Just knowing that you have an emergency plan can greatly alleviate stress.

Allow students to evaluate their own work or have them exchange papers to facilitate peer review. You may choose to use a short homework assignment or question sheet as a springboard for reviewing work or sparking discussion. The assignments used for these purposes need not be collected nor grades officially recorded.

Find classroom learning activities that keep students working cooperatively or thinking and writing independently, allowing time for you to interact one on one with them.

Observe students as they work in groups. When appropriate, grade them on what you saw or provide feedback regarding what you observed. Let them know that you will be watching them carefully; this will keep them focused and motivate them toward better performance.

If your school offers a photocopy service for handouts, avoid catastrophes by submitting master copies well ahead of time so that you have the papers you need at least a day early. Better yet, limit the need for distributed copies by using textbook-based assignments (if you have them), web-based assignments, or projected questionnaires.

Let technology work for you. This might include using Scantron® sheets for grading; professionally prepared teaching tools supplied by textbook or curricula publishers; educational Internet sites for images or video clips (save links for the good ones to reuse!); a good grade software program that backs up your data regularly; reputable (virus-free) online textbooks, digital study sites, instructional videos, and virtual activities; and online Bible study resources and daily devotionals for you or your church-school students.

## STUDY GUIDE FOR LESSON 5:
## THE DELIGHT OF DELEGATION

**1.** What is the most difficult part of delegation for you? Is it more difficult for you to delegate in your teaching role or in your personal life? Why?

**2.** When have you experienced challenges that were the result of botched delegation? What steps might you have taken to avert what probably felt like a disaster?

**3.** In Ephesians 4:11-12, Paul describes a division of labor that implies that Jesus' followers are not expected to "do it all" or operate in a vacuum of responsibility. Does this passage offer you a sense of relief or does it make you feel *more* stressed? Explain.

**4.** Read John 4. What do you find most striking about this encounter? Why?

**5.** Read Luke 6:12-16 and 8:1-3. What do you learn here about the people Jesus trusted? Do you think that Jesus' most-trusted friends ever disappointed him? Why or why not?

**6.** In the lesson, the author states, "Jesus was not a control freak." Do you agree or disagree? Why? Cite Scripture references to support your response.

**7.** In what ways does the need to control squelch the benefits of delegation?

**8.** List any tasks, job-related or otherwise, that you can appropriately delegate to others.

**LESSON 6**

# THE
# Force
## OF
# Focus

**Scripture Lesson:**
John 8:48-59
John 10:21-32
1 Corinthians 9:24-27
Hebrews 12:1-12
1 Peter 2:9-12

*"The only true wisdom is in knowing you know nothing. True wisdom comes to each of us when we realize how little we understand about life, ourselves, and the world around us."* —Socrates

It was a perfect, bright beach day with a light breeze and mild waves—which is probably why I didn't notice the long-shore current pulling me far from where my mom lay sunning. I swam awhile, bobbed in the waves, and then turned toward shore. Squinting against the sun, with salt stinging my myopic eyes, I could not see even a faint blur of our blue blanket or the yellow of Mom's suit. I rode a wave in, figuring I'd be washed up somewhere near where I'd entered the water, and was relieved to see a blue blanket not far from my landing.

Still squeezing water from my hair and winded from my swim, I plopped down on the blanket, which felt a bit softer than I remembered. "How's it going, Mommy?" I asked as I stretched out, dripping all over the blanket.

"It's going pretty well, but I'm not your mommy!" replied the stranger next to me, in a not-so-welcoming tone.

I was mortified! I was more than twenty years old, blind as a bat, disoriented, nearly naked, and completely helpless. I jumped up, apologized, and headed back toward water. If only I had worn my contact lenses, I'd be able to focus on shore and find my mom. But, alas, I'd left them at home, and as hard as I tried, I could not find her.

Terrified that I might sit on yet another stranger's blanket, I walked up and down the beach, squinting at every blue blur and cursing my helplessness. Finally, I heard my mom calling, "Suzy—over here!" Like a sonar-led bat, I followed the vibrations of her voice.

"Where have you been? I've been looking all over for you—I thought you were lost at sea!"

"Oh, I was lost, all right. You will not believe what I just did."

The importance of focus took on new clarity that day. The Scholastic children's dictionary's definition of the verb *focus* includes "to adjust your eyes or a camera lens so that you can see something clearly . . . to concentrate on something or somebody."

Great teachers focus on their students, their subject matter, and their skill set, but many share a higher focus—a focus on their God-given mission. Focus trains our minds, leads us toward action, and allows us to reach our potential. Focus keeps us on our chosen path despite distraction, resistance, or difficulty. Focus keeps us grounded and where we belong.

## Learning from Jesus

Jesus came to earth on a rescue mission. As his worldly résumé expanded (carpenter, itinerant teacher, rabbi, physician/healer, sacrificial lamb), Jesus remained focused on mission completion. How did he do it?

Jesus was aware of his mission and secure in his ability to complete it: "I have come to do your will, my God" (Hebrews 10:7) and "The one who sent me is with me; he has not left me alone, for I always do what pleases him" (John 8:29). The Lord's Prayer begins with his ultimate focal point: "Our Father in heaven, hallowed be your name, your kingdom come, *your will be done,* on earth as it is in heaven" (Matthew 6:9-10, emphasis added). And when it came to focusing on his mission, Jesus set his eyes, both metaphorically and literally, towards his Father in heaven. John 17:1 tells us that " . . . Jesus looked towards heaven and prayed: Father, the time has come. Glorify you Son, that your Son may glorify you. For you granted him authority over all people, that he might give eternal life to all those you have given him." That's quite a mission statement.

Scripture shows us a Jesus who successfully remained focused on meeting the needs of the people he came to serve and save as he moved towards successful mission completion. Spies once tried to trick him, hoping to turn Jesus over to the governor for seditious teaching (Luke 20:20-26). Instead of falling into their trap, Jesus taught them using an astonishing visual lesson: "Show me a denarius. Whose image and inscription are on it? . . . Then give back to Caesar what is Caesar's, and to God what is God's" (Luke 20:20-26). Even rock-wielding zealots couldn't distract Jesus from his mission—at least twice he was pursued by angry locals determined to stone him (John 8:58-59; 10:31-32). Can you believe that during one of these dramatic chase scenes, Jesus *pauses* to heal a man (John 8:58–9:7)? Think about it—would you have paused, or kept running from the fanatics trying to kill you?

Additionally, Jesus not only paused to touch and heal us, but he loved the people he'd come to serve. When Jesus advises the rich young ruler who wants to know the path to heaven (Mark 10:17-22), the Gospel text tells us that not only does Jesus answer the young man's question, but that he also looks at the young man and loves him.

Jesus was not only mentally/spiritually focused on his mission, but he also actively set himself on the mission completion course. When Jesus' formal teaching ministry was transitioning into his Judean ministry period, Luke tells us that "Jesus resolutely set out for Jerusalem." Literally, this translates to "Jesus set his face to go to Jerusalem." All along he must have known that it was in Jerusalem where he would later be betrayed and die, yet he remained determined to minister to those in the Judean towns and villages who would hear his message.

Jesus believed that all people could learn the lessons he came to teach. He refused to accept mediocrity from his students or from himself. Jesus instructed his followers to drop everything and simply follow—to follow their God-given mission with no looking back (Luke 9:57-62). Jesus spoke the hard truth and expected full commitment. He still does.

## Trying What Jesus Taught

Before you can focus on your mission, you first need to identify it. Do you believe like Jeremiah (Jeremiah 1:4-5) that before you were born, you were set apart by God and appointed to be a prophet—perhaps not necessarily a prophet to the nations, but God's representative to your school, your students, your athletes, your children? Or that like Esther (Esther 4:12-17) you have been placed in your position for such a time as this? The Psalmist, David, tells us (Psalm 139:13-16) that while we were still in the womb, God had already pre-ordained and recorded all the days of our lives. Let that staggering thought take hold: before your cellular differentiation and blastula involution, God knew you, loved you and had planned your purpose!

Is it your mission to serve God through serving others—sharing your knowledge and skills, empowering your students, lifting the helpless ones from the grip of poverty, ignorance, shame, or evil? Do you believe, like Mother Teresa, that "God loves the world through us" and that "if you can't feed a hundred people, then just feed one"? Perhaps you encounter God's needy creatures daily—and it is your mission to change the world one person at a time.

I didn't always feel sure that God wanted me in the classroom. In fact, it wasn't until a stranger asked me whether I had considered the mission field that I realized I was already on one! And, even after I realized that teaching was my mission, I was not always steadily fixed on my mission. It was easy to lose focus—I was distracted by financial questions, family issues, basic survival needs, and relationships.

After a few trying months of working with a difficult class, I was losing focus, feeling sorry for myself and sure that there was no reason to remain at Midway. Resentful that I'd lose yet another evening to grading, I sat down with the red pen. I was snapped back into focus when, at the bottom of a student's homework sheet, I read: "How do *you* think the universe was formed, Mrs. Drake? Do you believe in God and Jesus?" Hmm—maybe I do belong here after all . . .

At one point in my first year at Midway, I, along with all new teachers, received the dreaded pink slip. Budget cuts forced administration to let go all new hires—last in, first out, they told me. My dear colleagues, all seasoned teachers, gathered around me. I was stunned and hurt until the five men who made up the remainder of the biology department each vowed to give up one class assignment so that I could remain. "I feel like going part-time, anyway," one offered. "You need the job, and we want you here!" another added. Whoa—who had just fixed those corrective lenses onto my tear-stained face?

Sometimes God allows us small glimpses of his vision, sending us the corrective lenses through which we can refocus. The Lord's corrective lenses may take the form of questions from students, support from colleagues, or a stranger's comment. We might read a Scripture, a memoir, or a student's writing that inspires us. If you keep your eyes open, there's no telling what you might see.

## P.S. (PRACTICAL SUGGESTIONS)

Define your life's mission. Does it involve teaching, preaching, coaching, parenting, serving, performing, leading, following? Can you minister and love others through the role you are designed to fulfill? Consider your experiences and blessings as you honestly assess your gifts and current placement. Follow the example of

Fortune 500 companies and successful nonprofit organizations by developing and writing out your personal mission statement.

Review your mission statement at regular intervals, maybe every first day of the month. Revise your statement as needed (perhaps as God reveals and clarifies what you need to see).

Seek a crowd of witnesses who will support you as you pursue your mission. You might find like-minded believers within your social circles, your work environment, or a worship setting who are willing to hold you up in prayer or offer comfort, support, or a kick in the pants, as needed.

Be a spiritual coach or witness to someone else. God has designed the human experience to be one in which we support, complement, and partner with each other.

Like a ballet dancer who uses a focal point for balance and orientation while pirouetting, set your sights and soul on Jesus. Use his example as your set point as you strive to emulate his life and teaching.

Spend time daily in God's Word. Search the Scriptures for inspiration and guidance. Scripture promises that if we intently study and follow God's Word, our work will be blessed (James 1:22-25). Additionally, when we train our eyes and hearts on God and his will, we remain focused on our mission as the Holy Spirit fills us with the strength, comfort and wisdom.

Display Scripture verses that motivate you in your mission or help you focus on Jesus. Print them in an interesting font and post them in places you often view: the inside cover of your grade book, a corner of your bathroom mirror, or above your kitchen sink, for example.

Ask God for help. Jesus modeled otherworldly focus through life's difficult journeys. Even if things don't look so promising now, you know that it is God who has sent you, and only God defines your worth. Consider asking God for the focus you need to discover and accomplish your mission—and then be ready for an answer!

Consider your current state of physical comfort; how you feel may influence the quality of your teaching and your ability to focus. Then, decide what you can do to make yourself more comfortable or more physically fit. Could you use some hydration, a change of shoes midmorning, or a quick healthy snack?

Assess your spiritual growth. Consider finding a spiritual mentor or coach who can help you assess your progress. This person should be someone to whom you are responsible and with whom you might discuss Scripture and pray. Are you caught in habits or sinful thoughts that hamper your focus—behaviors or attitudes that keep you crawling when you should be running?

The next time a student drives you to distraction, why not try whispering a quick prayer in which you ask God for focus and redirection? Later, when you are more relaxed and focused, you can work out a plan to address the problem. In the tough moments, try to remember that Jesus came to serve *and* love.

Ask God to bless your work. Take to God your fears, concerns, and problem students. Lay your burdens down so that they don't obscure your vision.

Remember that, because you are a teacher, you are a leader. Your students, and the broader community, will notice your behavior and attitudes. They will look to you for more than the contents of your syllabus. Just as Jesus can serve as your model teacher, you will serve as a model to others. Ask Jesus to help you as you serve and teach in a way that will make him proud.

## STUDY GUIDE FOR LESSON 6:
## THE FORCE OF FOCUS

**1.** Define your mission by writing out your personal mission statement. On what or on whom should you be focusing at this point in your life?

**2.** What or who distracts you from focusing on those things you listed above? How might you manage those distractions?

**3.** Read Hebrews 12:1-12. How does this passage relate discipline to focus? Who can help keep you focused on your mission goals?

**4.** You probably know how difficult it is to maintain focus when balls are flying (too many in the air, lacrosse balls, spit-balls?). How do you suppose Jesus maintained focus in stressful and dangerous situations? See John 8:48-59 and John 10:21-32.

**5.** Read Hebrew 12:1-3. Sports metaphors resonated in first-century Rome much the same way they do in our sports-obsessed culture. The Colosseum games generated huge crowds, much like our stadiums do today. The witnesses described in Hebrews are our spiritual "home crowd." They root for us, they pray for us, and the leader of them all (Jesus) is cheering us on from the finish line. Use your imagination to create a mental picture of your crowd of witnesses. Who makes up this crowd? In whose crowd do you cheer, pray, and witness?

**6.** Which behaviors, habits, or thoughts hinder you as you race to your mission's finish?

**7.** The writer of Hebrews tells us to "cast off these so that we run well and with endurance." How does the endurance racer train and think differently from the short-event runner? How can endurance-training mentality be incorporated into our spiritual training and preparation?

**8.** When mountain biking on tight switchbacks in Colorado, my experienced cycling friends advised that I look ahead on the trail only to where I wanted my front tire to lead. Sure enough—if I looked at the sharp rock or the protruding stump ahead, I would certainly hit it and suffer the consequences. However, when I looked at the narrow opening where I wanted my front tire, my bike followed. Is there a spiritual lesson/metaphor here?

**9.** Which practical suggestion(s) are you willing to try?

# THE
# Dominance
## OF
# Demonstration

**Scripture Lesson:**

Mark 6:45-51

Luke 8:22-25; 19:1-9

John 6:16-21; 13:1-17

John 9:1-11

> *"The mediocre teacher tells.*
> *The good teacher explains.*
> *The superior teacher demonstrates.*
> *The great teacher inspires."*
> —*William Arthur Ward*

It's six in the morning. I'm stumbling down an embankment and feel my heel sink into something mushy. Hoping the mush is only mud and not dog doo, I forge onward and downhill toward the tiny stream. It's not really a stream, but more like a ditch filled with runoff from heaven only knows where. I'm practically downhill skiing in the layer of slippery, black goo. It's not until I'm "safely" in the ditch that I realize there isn't enough water down here for my samples. Climbing back up through the brambly grass on the steeper side, I grumble to myself.

Ah yes! I remember that there was a pond, of sorts, near my old apartment. Perhaps I can sneak onto the property and fill my sample jar there. A mad dash through the fence, one soaked leather shoe, and a muddy jacket later, I slide back into the driver's seat. Yahoo—looks like I've got some wigglers in my jar. Time for school!

Often, discourse is easier than demonstration. I could just lecture to my students on aquatic protists and avoid many hassles: lugging out all the microscopes, ordering slides, coverslips and dropper bottles, hiking down to the dirty old pond to get the water samples, and washing hundreds of slides. But, instead of observing wet mounts, my students would endure dry words and a far less memorable, less engaging lesson.

Another day, before the students partner up and find a quiet corner and a stethoscope, I demonstrate how to attach the blood pressure cuff, how to check the cuff and pump, and how to read the sphygmomanometer. Not until I'm done telling *and* showing them how to take each other's blood pressure with this equipment do I dare trust them to do it themselves. The effort of doing a short how-to demo helps to avoid many bruised arms, broken cuffs, and incorrect measurements.

Let's face it—in today's teaching arena, demonstrations work. The demo is usually relatively quick, resonates with visual and auditory learners, and is engaging, maybe even entertaining. My disengaged students sometimes wake up to watch!

How many times have *you* been in the classroom, prisoner to the droning, mind-numbing lecturer who is slowly driving you toward insanity? At some point you're mentally begging the professor to follow the Dalai Lama's advice: "Sometimes one creates a dynamic impression by saying something, and sometimes one creates as significant an impression by remaining silent." You want to stand up and scream: "Stop talking, now! Don't be vague. Stop blabbing on and on. I don't get it—just *show* me!"

## Learning from Jesus

Jesus understood the dominance of demonstration and active learning activities—he consistently used both. Jesus' entire life was a demo lesson. He came to teach us about the kingdom of God, so he *showed* us what a holy life looks like. Jesus' most memorable lessons were powerful demonstrations. These demonstrations were masterfully effective and engaging and efficiently communicated complex principles. Sometimes the demonstration *was* his entire lesson; other times Jesus followed his demonstration with a question-and-answer session.

"Look," Jesus says as he deftly unbuckles the strap and gently slides the crusty sandal off Peter's foot, "this is how you serve your brother." Despite Peter's objections, Jesus scrubs the sore, filthy feet of his friend. As the dead skin and dirt slough off into the basin, Peter and his friends begin to understand. The now odiferous, dirty rag is the teaching tool du jour. No other teaching technique could have taught as well as this practical and personal demonstration. Talk about getting "down and dirty" on the job (John 13:1-17).

Some lessons demand demonstration. Following the feeding of the five thousand, Jesus sensed that his disciples were confused, possibly even doubtful, about the day's events. Instead of once again explaining his divinity, chastising his friends for their doubt, or launching into a lecture on faith, Jesus walked about three miles (did you ever realize it was *that* far?) on top of the water before getting into the boat with them (Mark 6:45-51).

As an alternative to lecturing the lepers who approached him outside of the city borders, Jesus demonstrated power and compassion by healing all ten of them (Luke 17:11-14). Rather than delivering an artfully crafted "Power of God" speech, Jesus emptied Lazarus's tomb, calling his friend from death's grip (John 11:17-43). When asked how we should pray, Jesus *demonstrated* how we are to pray, speaking the words of the model prayer now known as the Lord's Prayer (Matthew 6:9-13). Even his closest followers didn't grasp the magnitude of Jesus' power until they saw him quiet a storm with his mere words (Luke 8:23-25).

Jesus substituted a sermon entitled "Loving and Accepting Sinners" with attending a dinner party at Zacchaeus's home. There, Jesus happily dined with his host of dubious reputation (Luke 19:1-9). On one particular Saturday, the Pharisees tried to draw Jesus into a debate on Sabbath law. Rather than arguing or offering an interpretation with which they could accuse him, Jesus answered their question with demonstration—the Pharisees watched as Jesus healed a deformed man in the temple, *on the Sabbath* (Mark 3:1-6).

After conquering death, Jesus still wasn't finished teaching. Following his transfiguration, Jesus appeared several times to his followers. The first time Jesus appeared to his disciples, they were terrified, thinking he was a ghost. So Jesus ate a chunk of bread— a simple demonstration that allayed their grief and fear, assuring Jesus' friends that he was not a ghost but their risen Savior.

Jesus also understood the importance of actively involving his students in the learning process. Numerous examples are found in the Gospel text, including Jesus' healing of a paralytic who is lowered through a roof during one of his more well-attended lectures. Jesus interrupts his sermon to heal the man and then tells him to walk and sin no more. When Jesus restores sight to a blind man, the man's healing is not complete until he follows Jesus' instructions to wash in the pool of Siloam (John 9:1-7). Another time, Jesus tells a paralyzed beggar, "I tell you, get up, take your mat and go home" (Luke 5:22-26). To the adulteress whom Jesus saves from stoning, he says, "Go now and leave your life of sin" (John 8:11b).

## Trying What Jesus Taught

Engaging students in active learning and using demonstrations to teach content requires additional planning and involves risk. Our lesson plans might not work as intended—we could overestimate the intellect of our students, choose the wrong demo, or experience sabotage. We might do a lot of planning and preparation for a small learning return. So many things could go wrong—and changing old routines can be stressful and downright scary. But the demonstration could also be a huge success—and a core component of your teaching repertoire.

"Does exercise change your blood pressure?" The third time I heard this same basic question in one day finally flipped me over the edge. My classroom is located at the end of the science wing, the closest room to a non-alarmed exit. And as long as you remember to prop open the door (illegally), you can get back in, so . . . "If you've all taken your blood pressure already, let's go see" was out of my mouth sooner than I had time to rethink the activity that I'd planned to do. I'd almost bailed on the idea of incorporating a before-and-after-exercise blood pressure measurement in our cardiovascular health lab. Who in their right mind would lead thirty-some students outside to run around? They barely made it into class, and the chance of getting them all back inside was best not considered. "Let's run around for a while, then come back in to retake our pressures and see," I challenged. The half-green, half-baked grass beckoned the runners. Leading the throng, I doggedly jogged despite my red heeled pumps. The class mostly followed, but within minutes I saw two young men break off from the group and gallop right off of school property. Their figures became smaller and smaller as I yelled more and more loudly, "Get back here, NOW!"

Then the unthinkable happened. Ramada, a plump, young lady with a reputation as a drama queen, crumbled to the ground under a tiny fledgling of a maple tree. The tree bent and swayed as she leaned against its puny trunk, gasping and shrieking, "My arm, my left arm. It's burning. I'm gonna die!"

I was thinking less about the runaways now and more about contacting an ambulance. Ramada could be faking, but her skin color was a bit off, and I was in no mood to take any more chances. "Josh, call 911 now! Ramada, can you hear me?" Suddenly the wail of sirens filled the air. The paramedics couldn't possibly have made it that quickly.

Oh, thank you, Lord. It's my 5:45 a.m. wake-up call, and the sirens are nothing more than my new alarm clock. The whole nightmare has been just that. All this angst, and my day has not even started!

Right before bed, I'd been reading from the Gospel of Matthew. What struck me throughout the reading was how involved Jesus was with his students. Teaching wasn't something he did *to* them but was something he did *with* them. I wanted to follow his example, but perhaps this dream was a portent of things to come.

I had two options. I could take my dream as a warning and avoid the more active component of the cardiovascular lab, or I could just do it. The whole Jesus thing had gotten to me almost as much as the dream, so when my first student posed the question, "Does exercise change your blood pressure?" my decision was made. "Let's go see!" But, before we bounded outside, I reviewed the techniques for measuring blood pressure and demonstrated the proper use of the cuff and dial system. I also carefully laid out specific ground rules and the objectives of our experiment. To say that I was frightened of the possible consequences is an understatement. I was scared silly and didn't even need any exercise to raise *my* blood pressure. If the students didn't do something bad, the other teachers might think I'm crazy. Putting my reputation, safety, and comfort on the line to teach a concept in a less traditional, perhaps more effective way was a bit risky. What was I thinking?

The students did harass me for running in my red heeled pumps—something about not being in Kansas. I did wear those shoes in the real scenario. And some of the students barely moved when they were supposed to be running. But no one ran off, and Ramada expended an unusual and generous effort to raise her pulse and blood pressure. Fortunately, she did so without disastrous effects. Once back inside, the question previously posed was quickly answered, and the lab was dubbed a favorite. I was equally glad I had stepped outside of the lecture format and relieved that my nightmare did not come true.

Teachers demonstrate so much more than we plan. Our students consistently watch us and study us. Students of all ages notice how their teachers react to stress, injustice, and praise—their scrutiny is intense and their curiosity palpable. Can't you feel inaudible pleading: "Teach me how to live! Show me how to act like a real man or woman! Teach me how to make it in this world!" Our words *and* our actions demonstrate our beliefs. We would do well to heed the advice of St. Francis of Assisi, who advised, "Preach the gospel at all times, and when necessary use words."

# P.S. (PRACTICAL SUGGESTIONS)

Do not fear the demo! History's greatest teachers used demonstrations, and so should you. Be secure in yourself and your abilities. When doubt strikes or you wonder if the prep is worth it, practice it again. Remind yourself of Jesus' teaching example and ask God for his wisdom, protection, and provision. When you are secure in God's love, you can take risks and enjoy your work.

If large class size or equipment issues limit the type and number of hands-on exercises you can incorporate into your lessons, teach with demos. Sensory-rich demos are memorable, stimulating, and engaging for many students in a short time.

Tap your colleagues and search professional trade journals for demo ideas. Classic demonstrations are often presented in teaching periodicals or favorite lab publications. Sometimes, teacher's editions of classroom texts include demonstration ideas.

Take time out from your own work to observe experienced teachers. Can you visit veteran model teachers, maybe even attend a class off-site? If you witness a particularly effective demonstration, ask for permission to copy it and for preparatory suggestions.

When you develop or master a good demo, consider sharing it with others. You might pass along to your colleagues a short description of the demo and a list of materials, suggestions, and safety tips. Consider submitting your ideas to a professional journal or initiate a system by which teachers in your department can share demo materials and data.

Practice your demonstration before you present it to your students. Anticipate potential complications and plan ahead for those contingencies. Think about what you expect the demo to teach before using it. Consider questions you will ask during and after the demonstration. You also might develop a follow-up assignment to cement the knowledge your demo taught.

Be prepared! Allocate extra supplies for your demonstration. You may need to redo the demonstration, either because it didn't work or because it was so successful—don't be shocked if your students beg for an encore!

Know your limits. My colleagues start their first lesson of the year with a demonstration that involves setting their lab desks on fire. They swear that it generates excitement (I believe it!) and excellent discussion, and they pressure me to follow their lead. I'm clumsy with lighters, wary of fire, and freakily safety-conscious, so I use alternative, yet effective demonstrations that day.

If at first you don't succeed . . . If you followed the guidelines above and your demo didn't work at all or failed to engage your students, don't despair. You may just need more practice. As you become more experienced and confident with your demos, you may find yourself excitedly enthusiastic for the lessons in which you use them.

## STUDY GUIDE FOR LESSON 7:
## THE DOMINANCE OF DEMONSTRATION

**1.** Think back to your days as a student. What was the most engaging or memorable demonstration you ever witnessed?

Why was this particular demo so good?

Did the demo you described at left reinforce something you already were familiar with, or did it allow you to learn something completely new?

**2.** Which demonstration do you most enjoy performing for your current students?

Why is it your favorite?

**3.** Read about Jesus' lesson on service in John 13:1-17.

What made this lesson so poignant?

**4.** Check out John's account of Jesus walking on water (John 6:16-21). What did this demonstration teach?

Not all demos are easy—consider that Jesus walked *three to three-and-a-half miles* over rough water for this one!

**5.** Remember those Talamini boys from lesson two? Do you suppose the empathy they embodied and their sacrificial nature developed in a vacuum? Their godly parents, Carol and Mark, demonstrated service to their boys and set high expectations for their sons.

Because Jesus planned to eventually leave the business of performing miracles to his disciples, it was important that Jesus provided them with demonstration-based training. Read the account of one such demonstration in John 9:1-11. Did Jesus *plan* this demonstration of God's power? Explain.

Which elements of this demonstration made it highly effective?

**6.** Is there any subject matter you currently teach that would be enhanced by a demonstration?

Where might you find ideas for these potentially enhancing demos?

**7.** Which of the practical suggestion(s) will you embrace?

**LESSON 8**

# THE
# Muscle
## OF
# Meditation

**Scripture Lesson:**
Joshua 1: 8-9
Psalm 1:1-3
Psalm 19
Psalm 77:12
Psalm 104:33-34

*"Wisdom begins in wonder."* —*Socrates*

"What I wouldn't give for a nice long nap!" My colleague's words echo my own deep desire. My foggy mind reaches back to Maslow's hierarchy of needs. Have I been meeting those needs, and what are they, anyway? For a brief but judgmental moment, I hope that I don't look as tired as Amy—her bloodshot, baggy eyes are not pretty. I briefly consider giving her a lecture about potential consequences of ignoring self, warning that she could easily become depressed or sick. It's obvious that Amy needs a hug and a snack more than she needs the lecture, so I pull out a bag of whole grain pretzels from my snack stash and listen.

"I just can't find the time for myself anymore. I mean, between taking care of my students, their parents, the administration, my planning, grading, and the teaching, not to mention my family's needs, I can barely keep my head above water," my beloved friend whispers. "Time with God? Time at the gym? Adequate rest? You've got to be kidding."

Gautama Buddha advised, "To keep the body in good health is a duty . . . otherwise we shall not be able to keep our mind strong and clear." And he continues, "Meditation brings wisdom; lack of meditation leaves ignorance. Know well what leads you forward and what holds you back, and choose the path that leads to wisdom." Ah—the media, the government, our doctors, Buddha—everyone tells us that we have to take care of ourselves if we expect to take care of others. You may have already discovered that this order is easier said than done. Sure, such advice sounds reasonable and holds a special allure, but how does that play out in the real world?

When done correctly, meditation can leave one rested and serene. The times that I've tried to meditate, however, I either spend most of my energy mentally finalizing the week's menu and grocery list or I fall asleep. So much for serenity and enlightenment.

The English word *meditate* is derived from the Latin base *medicus,* meaning "doctor," which leads to the verb *meden. Meden* translates as "I healed," and is related to the term *meditan,* meaning "I thought over." Even the word's Latin origins, then, suggest that meditation is reflective, healing, and relatively active. In *Celebration of Discipline,* author Richard J. Foster defines Christian meditation as the ability to hear God's voice and obey his word. Rather than focusing on a mantra or pursuing "esoteric flights into the cosmic consciousness," Foster suggests practicing prayer combined with quiet reflection, using our imaginations to make God's message come alive.

## Learning from Jesus

The Bible has a lot to say about meditation and clearly endorses it. Various Scriptures discuss the benefits of prayer, meditation, study, memorization, worship, fellowship, and solitude—and all are presented as critical to building Christian character. Thanks to the New Testament Gospel record, we can examine Jesus' commitment to these disciplines and explore the ways in which Jesus practiced meditation in his daily life.

The Muscle of Meditation

The Gospels describe a Jesus who recognized the need for down time. Although the bulk of his teaching was crammed into three busy years, Jesus didn't teach, preach, and heal nonstop— Jesus carved out time when he could be away from the noise and the crowd. In some accounts, we learn details of Jesus' meditative practices, but in others we are simply told that Jesus went off alone, or that he went into the wilderness, or that he went up on a mountain with so-and-so. This pattern of retreating indicates that Jesus had a unique understanding of his human condition and his own basic needs. Time and time again, Jesus disappears from the crowds for rest, time with Father God, solitude, or the comfort and support of close friends.

Before selecting the twelve apostles and beginning his three-year ministry tour, Jesus was led by the Spirit into the desert to be tempted by his adversary, the devil. Jesus prepared his mind, body, and spirit through the self-discipline of fasting. "After fasting forty days and forty nights, he was hungry" (Matthew 4:2). Talk about understatement! When was the last time you took forty full days to pray, fast, and meditate? Even by first-century Palestinian standards, forty days of food deprivation must've seemed a bit excessive. Who was managing Jesus' day planner?

On another occasion, after a long waterside teaching day, Jesus tells his disciples to take him to the other side of the lake. "Leaving the crowd behind, they took him along, just as he was, in the boat" (Mark 4:36a). After miraculously feeding five thousand of his students, Jesus dismissed the crowd and went up on a mountainside to pray (Mark 6:45-46). And, after hearing of his cousin John's death, Jesus "withdrew by boat privately to a solitary place" (Matthew 14:13). After another long day, Jesus turned his attention to his apostles: "Then, because so many people were coming and going that they did not even have a chance to eat, he said to them, 'Come with me by yourselves to a quiet place and get some rest'" (Mark 6:31). These instances indicate that Jesus retreated for at least five reasons: to refocus, to pray, to mourn, to rest, and to eat. Maybe every now and then, Jesus just took a nap.

Sometimes Jesus went into the wilderness alone, and at other times he went away with someone else. Matthew's Gospel recounts several situations in which we see a solitary, meditative, quiet Jesus. In Matthew 14, we read that Jesus went to a solitary place—he withdrew from the crowds. In Matthew 8:1, the account reads, "Jesus came down from the mountainside." There is no mention of anyone else coming down from the mountain with him, leading us to surmise that he had been up there alone.

In Matthew 24, we see Jesus sitting on the Mount of Olives. Again, there is no mention of anyone else around. How did Matthew know that Jesus was there? Other references specify the sites of Jesus' retreats as being solitary or mountainous. Jesus was doing a bit of mountain climbing, don't you think?

What about evidence of Jesus retreating in the company of others? Luke records a corporate retreat, telling us that Jesus took three friends, Peter, John, and James, with him up onto a mountain to pray. Isn't it interesting that the disciple who records this prayer meeting was not part of the foursome? Luke tells us that that they were gone until the next day, when they "came down from the mountain" (Luke 9:28-37).

As for Jesus' fitness level, few words speak volumes. Check out the casual reference to a long journey (on foot—no cars, Amtrak, or Megabus in those days) mentioned in Matthew 15:21: "Leaving that place, Jesus withdrew to the region of Tyre and Sidon." Matthew presents this journey as a non-event, barely mentioned—it probably didn't even make Jesus' master schedule. Yet when was the last time you walked the distance between central New Jersey and New York City? I don't know about you, but if I'm planning any physical endeavor of this magnitude, I'll be training for months and signing sponsors. The event would be a grand adventure, worthy of more than one measly verse!

Mark writes about Jesus' early morning meditation in such a matter-of-fact manner (in the same way that Matthew barely mentions the major "Walkfest") that we assume that morning meditations were part of Jesus' routine. Mark tells us that while staying at a friend's home, Jesus got up early in the morning, so early that it was still dark, and left the house to go off and pray by himself (Mark 1:35-37). How did Mark, the author of this account, know where Jesus was going or what he was doing there? Maybe Mark rolled over when he heard Jesus rising and pulled the blankets over his head with a groan. Then, after the disciples found Jesus later that morning, Mark asked Jesus what he had been doing out there.

Or, perhaps when Mark heard Jesus rustling around, he stealthily arose from his own mat and followed Jesus. It's also possible that Mark had already learned from Jesus the importance of morning meditation and was up before dawn looking for a quiet place of his own by the water.

The concept of morning devotions originated long before Jesus modeled them for us. Israel's King David considered morning a good time to meditate and pray. Psalm 5:3a records, "In the morning, Lord, you hear my voice; in the morning I lay my requests before you." Just because morning worked for Jesus and for King David doesn't mean it will work for you. If you're one of those people who can't even focus your eyes before 9 a.m., you might need an afternoon or evening quiet time.

## Trying What Jesus Taught

Serving as a Young-Life Saranac camp counselor was a great adventure and privilege, but the mornings there were a bit of a shock to my twenty-something self. I was so irked that every counselor at this Christian camp was required to attend daily early morning congregational prayer and Scripture readings. I couldn't believe that we had to assemble before the campers (who had giddily kept us awake most of the night) awoke. I thought that a bit more sleep would benefit me more than any unnecessary, ill-timed meeting and couldn't imagine how the older volunteers were managing to keep their eyes open and thoughts focused. It was during those sessions, however, that *my* eyes were opened like never before to God's vision. I learned from those determined, seasoned Christian workers; my perspective was re-aligned and my soul was fed. Drawing on God's power during these meditational assemblies proved to be a quite necessary key to surviving that week!

Morning meditation does work for a lot of people. The idea of putting aside some quiet time before the distractions and demands of the day hit is worthy of consideration. Additionally, *any* time in any context (solo or congregational) used to pursue God and listen for his voice is time well spent.

What moves you to contemplate God's glory and hear his voice: an early morning swim or run, an after-work hike, music, prayer on a mountainside? I would love to start out each day with prayer on the beach, but instead I settle for a short Scripture reading over tea and breakfast before making my short commute to school. While teaching at Midway, I usually entered the shared student/teacher parking lot to find myself surrounded by the students' pimped-out hot rods and shiny luxury cars or the more practical, shabby autos belonging to staff. The vehicles filled with students pulsated with bass, emitting foreign rhythms. But *nobody* would be grooving quite like me—I'd drive into that lot with my rockin' worship music blasting through my speakers, prepping for a day of challenges, reminding myself (and everyone else within a hundred yards) that God goes with me!

"Holy, Holy is the Lord Almighty!" I'm meditating, but once again, I'm *not* doing a quiet time, I'm doing a loud time. It's a praise party in the garage, on the bike path, or wherever I happen to ride. Although I can't study God's Word while biking, I find that it is during my workouts that I can best hear God's voice. My most meaningful worship coincides with aerobic exercise and the not-so-quiet voice of Christian rock blaring through my iPod. I contemplate Scripture, pray, and, when I'm not yet in my target heart rate zone, do a fair amount of singing, too. My children find this amusing, although I'm guessing that around 5:30 a.m., my neighbors do not.

There are many routes and venues through which we can seek our Lord, but we must discern which time, venue, and practice works best for us. There is a time for study, a time for prayer, and a time to praise—but we must carve out the time and be committed to these disciplines. We may think that we are too busy to meditate regularly, but there is no better way to discern God's will, comprehend God's power, and access God's wisdom.

Jesus' three-year ministry was filled with constant activity and days surrounded by needy people and crowds of seekers. The many teachings and miracles recorded in the Gospels speak of a busy man who could not make a habit of wasting time. Logically, we surmise that the time Jesus spent in prayer and meditation was both effective and crucial.

If you think that *your* life is busy, consider that many of Jesus' activities were never recorded. John writes, "Jesus performed many other signs in the presence of his disciples, which are not recorded in this book" (John 20:30). And yet the authors *did* include accounts of Jesus going off to pray, to meditate, and even to nap! If Jesus needed time alone to think, meditate, rest, and pray, how much more important are these practices for us?

## P.S. (PRACTICAL SUGGESTIONS)

Make time each day for a morning or evening meeting with Jesus. If you don't already do so, you can start with a five- or ten-minute block of time in which you can pray, read, or meditate on Scripture. Choose a time when you are least likely to be disturbed— block it out on your calendar and use it. As your Christian meditation time becomes more familiar, you might view it like basic hygiene—you can't go out of the house without it!

Find a good devotional guide and use it daily. *Our Daily Bread* is a guide that offers succinct and scripturally based daily devotions. You can usually find a free copy in your church lobby or request a subscription from the publisher. Might I suggest another guide with which I'm quite familiar? Consider putting *Morning Meetings with Jesus: 180 Devotions for Teachers* on your bedside or breakfast table.

Attend or organize a congregational prayer and study group. If you are working in a church setting, perhaps meet with other believers serving in your ministry area: pray together before performing on the worship team, or call on God's power and wisdom before serving in the children's ministry. Meditate either alone or with an assembly before teaching, preaching, or leading in any capacity.

Find a small group fellowship where you can worship, pray, and grow.

Don't fear the weekend nap. Work it, baby, work it!

Write a meaningful Scripture verse on an index card and leave it somewhere you will see it often (taped to the front inside cover of your grade book, next to your computer screen, or on your bathroom mirror).

Practice praying during times of the day when your mind usually wanders. Use those otherwise wasted moments (waiting in the lunch line, standing at the photocopier, sitting in traffic) for impromptu prayer.

Try one adjustment to your daily life that will make you healthier (take a short, brisk walk after school, join a gym, go to bed early). If the change makes you feel better physically, mentally, or spiritually, consider making it a habit.

Check into your neighborhood, school, or church fitness facilities. Can you use their tennis courts, track, gym, or pool?

Consider attending a workshop or retreat that offers a chance to relax, pray, and meditate.

Read and study Richard Foster's classic Christian guide, *Celebration of Discipline*. Use the book to help you explore the Christian disciplines, identifying those that resonate with your spiritual needs and strengths.

## STUDY GUIDE FOR LESSON 8:
## **THE MUSCLE OF MEDITATION**

**1.** Describe the images you associate with meditation.

**2.** Do you accept meditation as an important and valid Christian discipline?

**3.** Israel's King David practiced regular meditation. Check the references below to discover those things on which he meditated.

Psalm 48:9

Psalm 119:9-15

Psalm 119:48

Psalm 119:97

Psalm 119:99

Psalm 143:5

Psalm 145:5

How does your image of King David meditating differ from or align with the meditation image you described in your response to question 1?

**4.** What obstacles prevent you from meditating regularly?

**5.** What form of meditation brings you closest to God?

**6.** Could prayer be a form of meditation for you? Explain.

**7.** How did Jesus teach the importance of meditation?

**8.** Which practical suggestion(s) will you try this week?

# THE
# Freedom
## FROM
# Fear

**Scripture Lesson:**
Psalm 139:1-12
Matthew 10:17-31
Matthew 14:22-32
Hebrews 13:6

*"There is nothing more dreadful than the habit of doubt. Doubt separates people. It is a poison that disintegrates friendships and breaks up pleasant relations . . ."* —*Gautama Buddha*

"Dear Lord," I pray as I stare down Devil's Crotch, "please help me survive this, and I'll never do anything so stupid again," I mutter under my breath. The double black diamond ski run really is named the Devil's Crotch, and once I'm at its summit, there's no turning back. Mineshaft sits to the right of me and Tom's Baby to the left—both are also rated double black. My husband, Chuck, has already disappeared over the edge, in more ways than one, and the steepness of the chute I've descended to reach this point makes turning back impractical. Why I let Chuck talk me into this I'll never know—he assured me that I could do this run with no problem! Clearly there was some serious pathology in our relationship.

It seems wrong to pray for deliverance when I'm responsible for my own predicament. But that doesn't stop me from praying—I need deliverance, and I need it now! I soon find myself careening uncontrollably through the narrow, steep chute. Less than a minute later, I'm immobile, staring downhill and shaking in terror. When I finally descend again, it's my face that braces my first, second, and third falls. The words I say as I wipe the snow from between my eyes and my glasses are fit only for the devil. I'm ashamed of myself—my skiing skills or lack thereof, my own gullibility, and my vulgar words. I also know that if I don't control my fear soon, I'll become either figuratively or literally paralyzed.

Another day, I find myself crouched on the floor, in the dark, whispering to the thirty or so teens who are packed into the prep room hiding with me. On the "code red" signal, I had covered the tiny windows on the classroom doors, pulled down the large window blinds, turned off the lights, checked that doors were locked, and silently herded my students into the tiny prep room adjacent to the lecture area.

Then we wait. My students know to be quiet and still—we've practiced this before, just in case . . . We wait and listen—will we hear gunshots? Will someone break through the glass window and shoot us? In what kind of world do we live? I smell their fear and a fair amount of adolescent funk. Their anxiety is palpable, but so is the feeling of a class united. This time it wasn't a drill and later we learn of an armed intruder. Nonetheless, thirty-three minutes after the lock-down, we're back "at it" and cleared for learning.

In retrospect, some of my wildest fears seem ridiculous—I mean, it's not like I'm a first-century Christian facing down hungry lions in the Colosseum. And so much of the fear I've experienced through my life is a result of self-inflicted circumstance—the knot in my stomach as I stand ready to launch my hang glider over the mountain's edge, the anxiety preceding delivery of the lesson for which I haven't properly prepared, or the sense of queasiness as I attempt to descend Devil's Crotch. Even more of my fears are unfounded and impractical—I waste time worrying about a situation over which I have no control.

Yet I know that there have been times that I've allowed fear to diminish my teaching or paralyze my effectiveness. The mental energy that I should have been using to design clever lessons or to work with students was wasted with worry over several students who frightened me. I wonder when one will pull out a gun from under their sagging pants or I simply fear what they plan to do next. Most importantly, I ponder how I can show them that I am not afraid of them—once they sense my fear, I'm finished!

Other times, my fears kept me from sharing God's Word: Really, I'm not qualified to teach Junior Church—I'm not properly trained and it's not my age group! There's no incentive for those students to listen to me—it's not like they will get a grade, a report card, or a parent report to motivate them toward participation and cooperation . . . And working in the church nursery? Out of the question! I'm truly afraid of very young children and worry about which diseases I might contract once I'm exposed to their pervasive, nasty bodily fluids.

Could some fears be good ones, leading us away from danger or providing the adrenaline to escape harm? Early in my teaching career, several concerned students took the time to teach me the proper response when hearing gunshots in the hallway. They instructed me to drop down quickly or to flatten myself against the wall and "suck it in." I was grateful for their instruction as it made me a bit more street-smart, yet today I still can't differentiate between the echoing sound waves of harmless firecrackers and actual gunshots.

Whether it is fear for my own personal safety, concerns about job security, fear of litigation, worries about what people might think of me, or the dread of losing control of my classroom, I am sad to say that I am not yet free of fear's grip. When I find myself restless, fixated on problems I can't seem to solve, or fretting over the parent-teacher conference scheduled for the next morning, my sleeplessness is bound to impair my functioning and effectiveness the following day. Unless I change my worries into prayers, fear needlessly steals my potential for resolution as well as my much-needed sleep.

Perhaps the emotion of fear is just one of those conditions that are parts of being human. Like pain, fear might move us from harm's way and toward safety. Perhaps fear is an emotion that God designed for our own protection. Yet the fear that rules our minds or deters us from pursuing God's will can't be good. Does Jesus have anything to say about fear?

## Learning from Jesus

*Strong's Concordance* references 516 verses containing the word fear. Why so many?

God designed us and, at some point, allowed fear into the human equation. The Scriptures advise us to fear God and God alone—this recurring theme is sprinkled throughout the words of the prophets, the Psalms, and wisdom literature. "Fear the LORD your God, serve him only and take your oaths in his name" (Deuteronomy 6:13). "Serve the LORD with fear and celebrate his rule with trembling" (Psalm 2:11). "The fear of the LORD is the beginning of knowledge, but fools despise wisdom and instruction" (Proverbs 1:7).

Clearly, to fear God in this sense is not about the raw angst or terror that incapacitates, but rather speaks deeply of reverence and respect. To experience and practice this form of fear will promote a sense of health, wellness, and security. In other words, we choose to fear God and reap the benefits.

Almost as often as the Old Testament Scriptures command us *to* fear God in this positive sense, Jesus tells us *not to* fear. The fear Christ speaks against is the negative angst or terror that can destroy us. Jesus consistently demonstrates a life that never acquiesces to fear yet consistently bends to the will of God.

Both by analysis of Jesus' life and by the study of his words, we can see that Jesus has plenty to teach us about fear. And he speaks and acts as one who has personally encountered, understood, and conquered his own fears. In human form, Jesus experienced fear. One could argue that unless Jesus experienced fear, along with all the other human emotions, he didn't truly experience humanity.

Jesus shows us that there is a difference between intentionally controlling fear and passively allowing fear to control us. He consistently demonstrated a life that never acquiesced to fear. If you check into the New Testament Gospel references, you will not find any recorded situation in which Jesus succumbs to fear. Jesus never avoided pursuing the will of the Father based on his own fear, never bailed on a responsibility because of fear, and never allowed fear to dominate him. Jesus didn't allow fear to alter his words or dilute his teachings. He was a man who lived free from the confines and restrictions of fear. Let's begin by looking at just a few of the incidents recorded in the Gospels that show how Jesus reacts to fear.

Regardless of the circumstances, Jesus spoke only truth and lived his life based on that truth. Examine the situation where Jesus speaks with the corrupt Jewish leaders. "You brood of vipers, how can you who are evil say anything good?" (Matthew 12:34a). Jesus' words to the Jewish leaders are far from flattering—not a respectful way to address these pompous religious leaders. A sniveling, frightened Jesus would never dare to utter these words, purposely provoking such influential men. Despite these men's political power and societal influence, Jesus was clearly not afraid of them or of what they could (and eventually would) do to him. The reality in which Jesus lived was one in which God reigns supreme and has complete control over everything. Jesus lived outside of the world's "matrix" and acted accordingly.

Jesus habitually told people to "not be afraid." In Luke 8:49-50 we read, "While Jesus was still speaking, someone came from the house of Jairus, the synagogue leader. 'Your daughter is dead,' he said. 'Don't bother the teacher anymore.' Hearing this, Jesus said to Jairus, "*Don't be afraid*; just believe, and she will be healed'" (emphasis added). When the disciples witnessed Jesus walking on water, they were terrified. Instead of saying, "Hey, look at me guys! I really am special. You might want to consider worshipping me!" Jesus' immediate response to his shocked friends was, "Take courage! It is I. *Don't be afraid*" (Matthew 14:27, emphasis added). Yet again, after the disciples witnessed his transfiguration, Jesus repeated this pattern as the disciples fell on the ground terrified. "But Jesus came and touched them. 'Get up,' he said. '*Don't be afraid*'" (Matthew 17:7, emphasis added).

TEACHER TRAINING WITH JESUS

"Don't be afraid" really was one of Jesus' favorite phrases. In Luke we hear Jesus say it again! "When Simon Peter saw this, he fell at Jesus' knees and said, 'Go away from me, Lord; I am a sinful man!' . . . Then Jesus said to Simon, 'Don't be afraid; from now on you will fish for people'" (5:8-10, emphasis added). Why did Jesus preface a mission statement with advice on fear? Rather than using their fear to manipulate people, Jesus' words indicate that he sought to alleviate the fear that he empathetically sensed. In the above situations, Jesus uses a tense of the word "to not fear" that implies continuity, not just a one-time fearlessness. His choice of tense itself, then, instructs us.

So far, it seems as though Jesus simply wants to dissipate our fears. But then, as we delve further into the life of Jesus, we find instead that Jesus really *understood* fear. Consider the emotions Jesus must've experienced in the Garden of Gethsemane, while he prepared emotionally for his death—he knew that he was about to be crucified and he was painfully aware of all that involved. So how did Jesus deal with the ground-hugging, breath-robbing terror of that night of blood, sweat, and tears? He brought his fear to the Father in prayer. In the garden of Gethsemane (Luke 22:39-44), Jesus experienced emotion so strong that he fell face down on the ground and sweat blood. Do you think this account is exaggerated for dramatic effect? Some theologians believe that Jesus experienced a medical condition called Hematridosis, a condition in which severe fear releases chemicals that rupture the capillaries of the sweat glands, releasing sweat that is mixed with blood. The medical documentation for this rare condition is sketchy, so perhaps the biblical account is figurative and meant to convey the intensity of Jesus' fear. Regardless of whether he truly sweat blood or just felt like he did, the emotion Jesus experienced was way beyond worry or neurosis—it was acute and warranted fear. Even in my scariest nightmares or my worst days, I've never sweat blood, either figuratively or literally.

Jesus' first-century friends were familiar with danger and lived in fearful times. Jesus never discounted their fear, but he did redirect it, once telling his friends: "Do not be afraid of those who kill the body but cannot kill the soul. Rather, be afraid of the One who can destroy both soul and body in hell" (Matthew 10:28). Jesus then reassured his disciples, "So don't be afraid; you are worth more than many sparrows" (10:31). Jesus also knew the havoc that fear could create in the human psyche (he is the Creator, remember?). Jesus taught that fear of others is not healthy, but that there is *one* truly healthy fear. You might prefer to call it "respect," but Jesus actually used the word "fear" to describe the attitude we should have toward God.

In Matthew 10, Jesus addresses his disciples before they leave on a long teaching journey. Jesus does not confuse wariness with fear. He does *not* preach against taking precautionary measures for their safety, but rather instructs his friends to be wary, careful, and shrewd. He tells them to be on their guard and even suggests that they travel without money. Was this advice purely meant to foster their reliance on God and his people or was it also meant as a way to guard their personal safety? In Matthew 10:16, Jesus tells his friends, "I am sending you out like sheep among wolves. Therefore, be as shrewd as snakes and as innocent as doves."

Jesus certainly taught his disciples to overcome fear and must've done a great job of passing on to them his deific perspective. The same men who ran in terror on the night that Jesus was betrayed and killed became a bold and determined group. Most died martyrs' deaths rather than renounce their teacher. Perhaps it was the teachings of Jesus, his example, and the imbuing of the Holy Spirit that allowed the disciples to control fear and keep it in its proper perspective. Years after Jesus' ascension, Paul's words to Timothy vividly reflect Jesus' attitude: "For the Spirit God gave us does not make us timid, but gives us power, love and self-discipline" (2 Timothy 1:7).

## Trying What Jesus Taught

We fear things that we don't understand. Matthew's Scripture tells us that when the disciples saw Jesus walking on water, they were terrified. Did they still not understand the power their teacher wielded? Do you understand the power available to you daily?

Perhaps impulsively, Peter called to Jesus saying, "Lord, if it's you, tell me to come to you on the water." When Jesus told Peter to come, Peter responded by leaving the boat and walking above the water towards Jesus. But, as soon as Peter noticed the wind (and maybe the depth of the waves and water?), he panicked and began to sink. Did he "see the wind" because he took his eyes off Jesus? The moment Peter tasted fear, he started to sink. The text, however, tells us, that *immediately*, Jesus reached out his hand and rescued Peter.

You've got to wonder why Peter asked to join Jesus out there: was Peter trying to show off to the other disciples or was he just curious to test out his own belief. Notice that Jesus did not question Peter's faith until AFTER he'd rescued the man.

Would we live differently if we comprehended the full power of Jesus to rescue us? If we recognize that even if we do sink, Jesus will immediately reach out—that we will be ok *even if* that sneaky student doesn't like us, *even if* we walk through the valley of the shadow of death, *even if* we make a mistake, *even if* we lose everything? Recognizing that Jesus is there to rescue us even if . . . gives us a freedom from fear that makes our witness incredibly powerful.

I do not believe Jesus would ask us to take unnecessary risks, because he truly cares about us. But, I do believe that he wants us to live outside of fear's boundaries. Would Jesus begrudge you the extra five dollars you pay to park in the lighted garage when you have a late-night conference in a dubious neighborhood? If you consulted him, Jesus might recommend leaving your classroom door open whenever you are alone with a student or suggest that you to engage in the buddy system when leaving work after dark. After we make wise decisions and proactively pursue reasonable safety precautions, Jesus wants us to lay our cares and concerns at his feet. He has charge of everything and is ready to immediately reach out to rescue us, even if . . .

# P.S. (PRACTICAL SUGGESTIONS)

Make every effort to be wary, careful, and shrewd. Take steps to protect yourself and your reputation.

Consider engaging in the buddy system when you leave school, especially after dark. Find someone to walk with you to your car. Find and use the safest parking space available.

Leave your classroom door open whenever you are alone with any student.

Consider drafting your own personal safety policy and follow it without exception. If a student asks you for a ride in your car, but you know doing so would put you at risk, you can truthfully say, "Sorry, I can't provide student rides. It's against my policy."

Check the safety restrictions or guidelines set by your school district or organization and be sure to follow them.

Find out if your institution provides a comprehensive insurance plan that includes coverage for legal representation and court costs. If your school, union, church, or educational organization does not offer such protection, consider purchasing your own policy—investigate plans offered by independent organizations like the Christian Educator's Association International.

Pray! After making wise, wary, and shrewd decisions, lay your worries at God's feet realizing that God is in charge of everything and we are not.

Ask others to hold you up in prayers. God hears the petitions of his people and responds to their prayers.

Don't discount the protection of God's angels. They are real and employed for your protection (Psalm 91:11; Luke 4:10). Some of us need them and benefit from their services more than others!

Consider expanding your self-defense arsenal. Local martial arts studios or police departments might offer short courses in basic self-defense that are inexpensive or free of charge. Be sure to tell the registrar that you are a teacher—maybe you'll get a discount.

Memorize Scripture. Recite Bible verses, either in your head or aloud, when you feel rattled or frightened. Some possible choices include Psalm 23 or 2 Timothy 1:7.

## STUDY GUIDE FOR LESSON 9:
## THE FREEDOM FROM FEAR

**1.** What is your greatest teaching-related fear?

Is this a rational fear?

**2.** Is there anything you can do to lessen the intensity of this emotion? What?

**3.** Write down on a piece of paper the fear you identified in question 1. Holding the paper in your hand, approach God in prayer. Ask God to take your fear. To signify your surrender and consequent freedom, when you are finished praying, rip up the paper or burn it.

**4.** Read Deuteronomy 6:1-15.
How does this text approach the concept of fear?

Read 1 John 4:13-18 and 2 Timothy 1:7-12. How does the
New Testament address fear?

**5.** Compare the Old Testament and New Testament teachings
on fear. Here are a few Scriptures to get you started:

| Old Testament | New Testament |
| --- | --- |
| Deuteronomy 6:13 | Matthew 10:16 |
| Psalm 2:11 | Matthew 10:28-31 |
| Psalm 139:1-23 | Luke 5 |
| Proverbs 1 | 2 Timothy 1:7 |

**6.** Jesus modeled freedom from fear. How does his example
honor the Old Testament Scriptures *and* teach of a new
beginning?

TEACHER TRAINING WITH JESUS

**7.** Are there steps you can take to increase your safety quotient? What are they?

**8.** Choose the practical suggestion(s) that will help free you from the confines of fear.

**LESSON 10**

## THE
# Power
## OF
# Perspective

**Scripture Lesson:**
Psalm 39:1-4; 147:15
Ecclesiastes 3:1-15
John 1:1-18
2 Peter 3:8

*"It's not that I'm so smart, it's just that I stay with problems longer." —Albert Einstein*

Often, attitude makes all the difference—and attitude is driven by perspective. Webster's definition of perspective includes "the capacity to view things in their true relations or relative importance." Who aligns your perspective—students, neighbors, family, the popular culture, friends, or God's Word?

My attitude toward my teaching career occasionally takes a turn toward the bitter, my perspective twisted by a society that tells me that I am wasting my time and am ill-compensated for my hard work. I focus on my debts instead of my blessings, my limitations instead of my opportunities, and my weaknesses instead of my strengths. Until I fix my eyes on Jesus, I see only obstacles and temptation. In the same way that my body responds to regular chiropractic care, I also require routine perspective adjustments.

There was the day that my student, Tracey, rescued me from mission free fall. I was spent, utterly exhausted, and ready to quit—the students in my fifth-period class were wearing me down. But Tracey patiently waited after class until everyone else had disappeared. "Mrs. Drake, I apologize for my classmates. They're acting stupid and trying to drive you out like the last three teachers we've had. I won't let them. I'm going to get them in line for you. Please don't go!" she pleaded.

Another time I read the following comment on an end-of-year evaluation: "You are such an intelligent woman. I don't understand why you don't pursue a career in medicine or law. Why do you keep teaching?" Pondering these words, I first felt flattered, then uncertain before eventually remembering my mission from God Almighty! And you are on God's mission, too. Regardless of whether you are teaching, leading, singing, preaching, coaching, tutoring, parenting, or changing diapers and wiping drool, you are serving in Jesus' name.

As useful as Tracey was in realigning my errant attitude, others were equally destructive. The student who told me I was wasting my time, the neighbor who looked down on my "naïve idealism," and a close friend who dismissed my paltry teacher pay. So how do you filter meaningful messages from harmful hubris? What drove the world's greatest teachers to mission completion?

Socrates took the hemlock (as punishment for his public teachings), rather than the advice of his opinionated, younger wife. Rumor has it (and historical documents back up the gossip) that Socrates's wife, Xanthippe, loudly voiced her opposition to his career choice. She would have preferred to share the earnings of a doctor or lawyer, and she told Socrates so. Did Xanthippe look down on Socrates because he could barely support the family on a teacher's salary? The barter system that students compensated Socrates with was hardly regular or respectable income. It was bad enough that Socrates had taken a personal vow of poverty, but what's a girl to do when the children need shoes?

Yet Socrates believed that his career was one of a higher calling. He believed that it was his life's mission to seek, teach, and discuss truth. Like Jesus, Socrates saw ignorance as an enemy and his role in eradicating it as a sacred duty. So Socrates continued to teach in the marketplace rather than shop there.

We might intellectually recognize our work is a sacred duty, yet occasionally lose sight of our higher calling, distracted by challenges and expectations of how we think things should be. Like the day that Q came into class, with a chip on his shoulder and a bag of them in his backpack. I'd been going out on a limb to help Q—he came to my ninth-grade class mid-year, I wasn't sure if he could read, his attendance was spotty, and he was often late to class. But he was respectful and responsive to my efforts to help him tackle the introductory biology I was tasked to teach him and I enjoyed his quick wit and gentle spirit. I met with him after class to give him extra help, conferenced with him and his mom, and developed a plan to help him succeed.

I wasn't surprised when, deep into testing season, Q sauntered in late to class and sat down to open his backpack (for the record, school policy bans backpacks and food in the classroom). I *was* a bit taken aback when Q removed a bag of chips from his backpack, loudly opened the bag, and then decisively and overtly moved those chips slowly into his mouth—one by one he held them up for all to see, popped them into his mouth and crunched loudly. This behavior was somewhat out of character—not the Q I already adored. Since Q was flagrantly violating two school rules I had to say something. So, I was *quite* surprised when Q's response to my "Please put away the chips and focus on the lesson, Q" involved Q telling me to &#@% myself. He followed this uncharacteristic outburst with a hasty exit, a slammed door, and another crass reminder of what I should do to myself. I stood there feeling shocked, betrayed, insulted, and frantic to re-establish classroom order. The remaining students looked to me—I can only imagine what was going through their minds. I know what was going through mine: "Why am I here serving students who don't care about themselves, let alone me? They don't appreciate my efforts and devotion—I hate this job!" My perspective was quickly twisted . . .

Before day's end, Q returned to me with a sheepish look and an apology. He explained that he'd been testing for hours before arriving late to class. "Mrs. Drake, I was hungry and so tired—when you asked me to put away the chips, I just snapped." I accepted Q's apology, thanked him for explaining, and assured him we were "all good." Much later I learned that Q's home-life situation was beyond dysfunctional—that school was the only place he could relax and feel secure. Maybe those chips were the only food he would enjoy that day . . . after hours of testing. In the end, my relationship with Q was restored, my perspective was re-aligned, and I re-established a sense of mission assurance.

## Learning from Jesus

Jesus was not just about training—he was also about calling. "Come to me and I will give you rest." "Follow me and I will make you fishers of men." When Jesus called his disciples, he could have chosen men who were already learned and great teachers. Such men could have made quite an impression in the temples and public forums. But the men he called as his first disciples were Peter, James, and John—perhaps stinky, relatively uneducated fishermen. Eventually these men became great teachers and leaders who forever changed the world. Instead of calling the trained, Jesus trained those he called.

Jesus understood time and its fleeting nature. His teaching ministry did not officially begin until age thirty and dramatically ended with his crucifixion at age thirty-three. His career kick-off involved a wedding feast and production of some very fine wine. Jesus spent a lifetime preparing for a ministry that he knew would be a short one. Jesus reminded the disciples frequently that he would soon leave them. When we compare our lives with the endless stretch of eternity, our teaching seasons are limited, too.

Christ did not collect a CEO salary, vest in a 401(k), fly business class, or stay in five-star hotels. He did not solicit contributions during his teaching tours but allowed a cash-strapped woman to dump rare and expensive perfume over his feet. Jesus lodged outdoors or in friends' homes and fed on fish and faith. During his ministry, Jesus and his disciples lived simply, accepting food, lodging, and travel funds from friends. Jesus most likely experienced uncomfortable sleeping arrangements (Luke 9:58) and missed meals as he and his entourage traveled from town to town.

God's economy is different from ours. In God's view, a widow's last copper coin is worth more than a rich man's hefty contribution (Luke 21:1-4). Instead of portraying wealth as a right or necessity, Jesus warned at least one rich man of wealth's liability and potential complications. He told his disciples that "It is easier for a camel to go through the eye of a needle than for someone who is rich to enter the kingdom of God" (Mark 10:25). However, Jesus followed this dire warning with a promise of hope: "With man this is impossible, but not with God; all things are possible with God" (Mark 10:27b).

## Trying What Jesus Taught

Sometimes we need a reminder that the Master of the Possible is always on our side. Perhaps you will hear God's voice speak mightily in the fire or wind. Or his intentions may be revealed in a quiet, discrete declaration of whispered truth.

Fighting back tears of anger and confusion, I stood helplessly, surrounded by the usual bedlam of the main office . . .

Jesus, help me. I can't believe I'm here in this place. I try to be a good person. I have a good education, have been awarded all kinds of academic honors, and have traveled all over the world. But, instead of being in some mahogany-paneled boardroom or lunching in a trendy restaurant, here I am, surrounded by derelicts with the intelligence of pond scum. Their mouths are foul, they carry weapons, they sneak out to do drugs, and I can tell that that group over there just made some rude comments about me as I walked past. What kind of fool am I? I *should* have gone into law or medicine. Why am I here? And then God spoke.

*I want you here.*

TEACHER TRAINING WITH JESUS

Why can't I just go to Africa or become a missionary on some tropical island or something? At least then I would feel like I was doing something for you.

*You* are *doing something for me. I need you here.*

Why here? What can I do that any other teachers can't, and what person in their right mind would want to teach here anyway?

*I need you* here *to feed my sheep.*

Sorry, Lord—the closest things I have to sheep are the hearts in the bucket behind my room for next Thursday's dissection lab. And I sure won't be feeding them anytime soon.

*You know who I mean. And it doesn't hurt to pray for those kids you just thought of as pond scum. You know, I made pond scum, too, and it really is quite interesting. If you would just decide to love these kids, I'll help you do it.*

But they are so hard to love!

*And you think you weren't. I managed to endure more than an unpleasant walk in the hall for you.*

Well, it's just that my whole life seems consumed by this job. I definitely don't get paid enough to put up with all this. Should I really spend my precious time scrubbing desks, cleaning test tubes, and standing mindlessly in front of a copy machine?

*I washed stinky feet and rode around on an old donkey (and that was on a good day).*

And what kind of thanks do I get from these kids—or from the administration? Can you believe that I called down for a principal when that hoodlum threw a punch at Alex, yet they didn't do a thing?

*I know what you mean. The authorities never did much for me either.*

The students don't want to learn, and I'm starting to feel like it isn't worth trying to teach them. Half of them have parole officers and the other half should.

*When I frequented Jerusalem, they tried to give me a parole officer too.*

Oh, come on, get serious, please! I'm feeling seriously sorry for myself right now, and you're not helping me much.

*I will help you if you let me. You already have my Spirit and my power. All you need to do is share it and do your job with joy and love. I'll take care of the rest. You're the one for this job. I decided a long time ago. Because you are my child, you have many traits that make you suited for this job.*

Sure, a death wish!

*Well, sort of. Remember to live for me is life and to die is gain. So you don't have to be paranoid about everything that you see and hear. Trust me to watch out for you. I always care for my own. But you should learn to be observant and do what you can about the injustice around here. Open your eyes. Can you see the pentagram on that boy's notebook? Pray for him now!*

Okay . . . I guess you know about the drive-by shooting last week, too. I can't believe that they sounded a fire alarm and we all stood out by the curb waiting to be shot. That didn't seem to make much sense. And I had no idea what was going on.

*Did you get shot?*

No—but this job is really tough. I'm up half the night grading papers and planning classes. I'm awake and reading past midnight trying to stay one day ahead of the students. When I finally get to sleep, I have "bad class" dreams and wake up in a cold sweat. I'm a tired mess with a bad attitude!

*I'm happy to help with your perspective issues but I have even more to offer—Come to me, and I will give you rest.*

Oh, I'm ready for a good long rest!

*Not yet. You still have to teach your fourth-block class. I know that kid Mohammed is driving you nuts. But I love him so much. Don't forget, you are my messenger. Now, go before you're late.*

## P.S. (PRACTICAL SUGGESTIONS)

Display a reminder that speaks of time's fleeting nature. A highly visible sign posted directly under your classroom clock that reads, "Time will pass. Will you?" might remind both you and your students that time is limited and important. Or, you might choose to start each class with a moment of silence or a routine that prepares you and the students to work hard. I don't teach Latin, yet I had fun with this little class-opener: I officially started each class session by shouting the Latin phrase "Mox nox en rem" ("Night approaches"). I trained my students to (enthusiastically) reply, "Carpe diem!" ("Seize the day!"). This lasted a few weeks . . .

Set your perspective. Spend time in prayer before outlining your personal mission statement. Writing out a formal mission statement will help you identify your goals and your strengths.

Ask God to help you see your students, family members, colleagues, and superiors through his eyes. Ask for God's wisdom and guidance as you move through each day.

Instead of relying on the popular culture to determine your attitude and dictate your self-worth, search the Scriptures for God's perspective.

Confess. Guilt can cloud your vision and skew your perspective. Do you need to seek the forgiveness of a friend, family member, colleague, or student? Are there unmentionables that you still need to confess to God?

Forgive others. Grudges and bitterness can also cloud your vision. Ask God for grace and the ability to forgive those who have trespassed against you.

Ask a trusted friend to list your strengths and gifts. Ask them for an honest assessment. Then ask yourself if you are using your gifts and talents for *God's greater purposes*.

Take a drive or ride. Are you feeling poor while making more money than most of the families that your school serves? Take a drive or bike ride into the community—look around and count your blessings. If you see poverty, thank God for what *you* have and pray for your impoverished students. If you see opulence and wealth, thank God for being able to enjoy such an atmosphere, even if only during your workday.

Hike along a beach, a wooded path, or any natural environment where you might hear God speak. Worship there and allow God to align your attitude with his will.

Use your highest gift at work! Jesus taught his followers to use their God-given talents and gifts. Most people in corporate

America never get to use their highest gift at work. You, by contrast, are strategically and powerfully placed in a position that allows you to exercise your calling and giftedness every time you teach and serve.

Don't miss your Esther moments! Remember Queen Esther of Old Testament fame? When she was faced with a dangerous and frightening task, her uncle and guardian, Mordecai, advised, "And who knows but that you have come to your royal position for such a time as this?" (Esther 4:14b).

Open your ears and eyes. Perhaps you need realignment and will find it through the words of a student, teacher, or friend. Are there situations in which you can spread God's love, acceptance, or wisdom?

Check out Isaiah 40:12-17.

Ask God to reveal the wisdom and knowledge that will align your perspective. Consider how God answered Solomon: "Because your greatest desire is to help your people, and you did not ask for wealth, riches, fame, or even the death of your enemies or a long life, but rather you asked for wisdom and knowledge to properly govern my people—*I will certainly give you the wisdom and knowledge you requested*" (2 Chronicles 1:11-12, NLT, emphasis added)

When you feel unsure of your mission or doubt your ability or value, meditate on Jeremiah 1:5-9. Reference this passage when you need to re-align your perspective.

Memorize Joshua 1:9: "Have I not commanded you? Be strong and courageous. Do not be afraid; do not be discouraged, for the LORD your God will be with you wherever you go."

Rest. When all else fails, get a good night's sleep. Often, seemingly hopeless situations look better in the morning.

## STUDY GUIDE FOR LESSON 10:
## THE POWER OF PERSPECTIVE

**1.** Name the one person who most influenced your life.

**2.** What is your mission?

Write out your personal mission statement.

**3.** Identify and record your talents and gifts.

If you have trouble identifying your greatest gifts and talents, you might ask for insight from someone who knows you well.

Are you able to use your talents and gifts in your teaching?

**4.** Do you see your position as one of a higher calling?

Is it important to you that you use your gifts and talents toward God's greater purposes? How can this purpose alter your perspective?

**5.** Are there attitudes you carry that deter your teaching? If so, try to identify and list them.

Can God help you realign your attitude and perspective? How might this happen?

**6.** Read Esther's story, as recorded in the Old Testament book of Esther 1–8. If you prefer to watch rather than read, the VeggieTales version of the story is entertaining and as true to the Scriptures as any available vegetable-based rendition. Describe your latest Esther moment.

**7.** Jesus was all wisdom, knowledge, and power—his perspective was aligned with God's perspective. How can we align our perspective with God's priorities?

**8.** Which practical suggestion(s) will you embrace this week? This month? This year?

# Note
## FROM THE
# Author

*"No mind has imagined what God has prepared for those who love him."* —*1 Corinthians 2:9b*, NLT

I pray that you've found this study a helpful and provocative motivator. Thank you for taking the time from your busy life to consider these ten lessons and examine Jesus' teaching model.

I hope that you will soon find many opportunities in which to practice Jesus' ten teaching tips. If you like what you've read but feel that you've only skimmed the surface of a deep pool, please continue your study. There is so much more to discover—if you keep searching the biblical record, you will find so much more practical and time-tested teaching advice.

This can be just the beginning of your teaching-like-the-Master journey!

God bless,
Susan